One Sixth of a Gill

Jean Gill

Jean Gill's previous publications

Novels
Bladesong *(lulu)* 2012
Song at Dawn *(lulu)* 2011
Someone to Look Up To *(lulu)* 2011
San Fairy Anne *(lulu)* 2010
Crystal Balls *(lulu)* 2010
On the Other Hand *(Dinas)* 2005
Snake on Saturdays *(Gomer)* 2001

Non-fiction
How Blue is My Valley *(lulu)* 2010
A Small Cheese in Provence *(lulu)* 2009
Faithful through Hard Times *(lulu)* 2008
4.5 Years - war memoir - David Taylor *(lulu)* 2008

Poetry
From Bed-time On *(National Poetry Foundation)* 1996
With Double Blade *(National Poetry Foundation)* 1988

Translation (from French)
The Last Love of Edith Piaf - Christie Laume *(Archipel)* 2014
A Pup in Your Life - Michel Hasbrouck 2008
Gentle Dog Training - Michel Hasbrouck *(Souvenir Press)* 2007

Acknowledgements

A big thank you

to my editor, Claire, for her passionate belief in this book as well as her editing skills. Her input on trans-Atlantic differences was an education for me. 'I did not know that' is becoming my catch-phrase.

to those who've modelled for my photos, accepting all kinds of mad ideas and coming up with a few of their own. You know who you are.

to everyone in the Dieulefit Writers' Group. You've read some of these pieces hot off the press and your input has improved them and motivated me.

and to my criticial friends in the Hysterical Fiction group online. Your support is invaluable, professionally and personally.

Quotations taken from:
Mark Rowlands *The Philosopher and the Wolf* (p. 46), Granta. Kindle edition
Stephen Hawking *A Brief History of Time* (Bantam)

Jean Gill's translations from lyrics by Francis Cabrel and Jean-Jacques Goldman courtesy of Sony Music, France.

Pieces in this book have previously been published in *Not a Muse* (Haven Books), *Going Places* (Bridge House), *Poems for Year 4* (Macmillan), *Writers of the Year Competition Winners Anthology* (Writers Inc), *Night Balancing* (Blinking Eye), *The Poet's House* (Gomer), *Roundyhouse, Orbis, Pause* (National Poetry Foundation) and www.readwave.com

Praise for 'One Sixth of a Gill'

Unputdownable
'It is like having a conversation with a group of friends over dinner, where the topics wander and morph quite organically as occasions and images are recalled by the guests. The result is an eclectic mix which is quite unputdownable.

More than anything, I liked the way it was put together in a way which allowed for grazing or an all-out feast. I expect folk will keep returning to the table for a while after the final course.'
B.A. Morton, author of prize-winning crime novel 'Mrs Jones'

A rare treat.
'I dipped into your One Sixth of a Gill at the breakfast table, during siesta and sometimes before night-time sleep, which is how I think many readers will 'use' your book. And I do think it is a book to be 'used' – for its thought-provoking content, for some of its images that require scrutiny and interpretation. Some days I opted for a more superficial reading because daily life had its own measure of minor stresses and I needed no extra. On those days I loved the photographs, the dog tales, the knowing sub-text about marriage and parenthood.'
J.G. Harlond, author of 'The Empress Emerald'

A superb collection – so much variation in style and all equally brilliant. Thank you.
'What leapt out at me was the strong sense of colour in all your writing, especially the poems and stories. I wonder if that is because you are a photographer; you are very aware of it, pick up the nuances and you use this to brilliant effect in shading the writing with feeling. Your collection reminded me of a box of scarves we had in ballet class when I was young, all different shades and hues. I loved hunting through them and I guess that's what I'm trying to say about your collection. There is something for whatever mood you find yourself in.'
Karen Maitland, author of 'The Vanishing Witch'

For Lesley of Dieulefit

About the Author

Photo by Gary Martin

I'm a Welsh writer and photographer living in the south of France with a big white dog, a scruffy black dog, a Nikon D700 and a man. I taught English in Wales for many years and my claim to fame is that I was the first woman to be a secondary headteacher in Carmarthenshire. I'm mother or stepmother to five children so life has been pretty hectic.

I've published all kinds of books, both with conventional publishers and self-published. You'll find everything under my name from prize-winning poetry and novels, military history, translated books on dog training, to a cookery book on goat cheese.

My work with top dog-trainer Michel Hasbrouck has taken me deep into the world of dogs with problems, and inspired one of my novels. With Scottish parents, an English birthplace and French residence, I can usually support the winning team on most sporting occasions.

This book gives a taste of the whole range of my writing and includes much that is autobiographical and even more than usual that is from the heart. You will know what I mean as you dip into this collection. I hope you enjoy it.

Contents

Clearing Out

If Eric had not built the walk-in wardrobe, the rail would not have been high enough. It was sure to be strong enough though, as his DIY skills could be trusted completely. And of course the stool was neatly in place to enable her to reach the rail. Angela inspected each item of clothing in turn, starting with the crammed corner she never visited. Eric had asked her to clear out. She ran her fingers along the fabric of her life. A maternity dress, smocked and floral, that she'd kept, just in case. No chance of that now. Her graduation gown, still starched and smelling impossibly of pipe smoke and her tutor's study, a whiff of academic ambitions. Her wedding dress, a froth of lace.

She gave each item due consideration, made her judgement and moved on. She had always found it difficult to choose what to wear. She knew what she didn't want. Not black, not denim, not sexy. Well into the everyday section, she found what she was looking for. If she shut her eyes, she could still find it by following the faint trace of creosote from the time she painted the garden fence. There were even brown splashes on the blue quilting, in the shape of smiles. Her gardening coat had been battered by a million raindrops, scratched by a trillion thorns, kept her company for decades in moments of solitary peace. She took it from the hanger, slipped into its frayed lining, felt completely at home.

Then she found a scarf, tied it over the rail and noosed it round her neck as she stood on the stool, the one Eric had placed there for her convenience. When he found her, he would approve of the blue scarf - it matched her coat.

A Diamond for Valentine's Day

For Lauren

'**B**ring me a present,' said the princess, in reply to his proposal of marriage, 'and I will know what to answer you.' Then she was gone in a swirl of ambiguous rainbows.

His love was deep as caves and high as clouds so the dream-master searched his night world for the right gift. He saw a multi-faceted diamond that would sparkle like her beauty; a sensuous, full-bodied wine that tasted of her lands from grape to oak-aged maturity; a poppy seed containing all life's potential and fragility. Nothing said it all.

The possibilities grew beyond remembering and he knew he would lose her. He doubted himself. He doubted their relationship. If she was unsure, was it not already decided otherwise? What did she want?

And so he broke the laws of magic to spy on her where she lay and to raid her dreams. He was not in them, nor any man. She dreamed of what she could be, of what she could do, of where she could go to be her best self. He felt her fears and he understood.

On the due date, he stood before her, swathed in nebulae. 'This is the present,' he told her, opening empty hands to free the invisible bird and let her fly. 'Always free,' he promised her, a diamond glistening on his cheek.

'Yes,' she replied and kissed the diamond, another kind of promise.

Silk

You slipped me on you, easy
as a wedding ring along a finger's length.

After, I felt naked, more teased
than clothed by my kimono,

my landscape rivulets
of floral silk. My mother said

real silk slips through a wedding ring
so fine it is. I shivered.

When you colour-washed my clothes
the painted roses blurred. My artist,

brush my silk again; my lover
brush my silk.

Welcome Home

On tiptoe in blue ballet shoes
half holding
half holding back from
the breathing bundle on her mother's lap.
'This is your new sister,'
says her mother, queenly,
smocked in folds of fabric
stiff and floral in the sun.
'Your new sister,'
smiles Auntie Jo
but the smile is for the baby.
Floral hedgeballs line the path
in shadows to the outside gate
unlatched so often now for visits.
The skipping rope still lies
forgotten, yesterday's toy.
Her fingers interweave
a tiny fist; she wonders about
being a new sister.

Trying It On

I used to sneak into my sister's room
when she was out.
I pinched her lipstick, made my mirrored mouth
a cherry pout.

One time I found this bronzing tube and creamed
my spotty face.
By break I was a tan-streaked member
of the Asian race.

The Head was mad and wrote a letter home -
my Mam was tamping.
She banned me from the treasure drawers and
left me stamping.

She said, 'No more of that, young brazen Miss!'
(like brass, it means).
Instead I tried on heaps of sister-clothes,
her tops and jeans.

When I am sixteen I will be a model
look so ultra-cool.
It's not fair I can't have stuff of my own
to make boys drool.

I peeked in when our Anne was kissing Dai
just for some tips.
She caught me, threw a shoe and said,
You're pushing your luck, you are.'

tamping - Welsh dialect word for 'angry'

Cefn Sidan

Where skylarks vie with seagulls,
melodies with croaks,
sand drifts across dry grass
and wooden footpaths trail
ghostly as if undersea
to march again up the Worm's Head.
In clumps, the crowds define
their spaces on the beach with
strategic towels and picnic bags.
Carbon dioxide fizzes from a can
signed bright blue bright red Pepsi -
contents colourless.
I remember
dogs barking, fetching sea-spray
rubbing close then shaking off the mud,
to spot my clothes and skin
before the concrete toilets
designated this a blue-cross
no-dogs European tourist
canned beach.

Cefn Sidan is a beach in South Wales with a view across to 'the Worm's Head' of the Gower Peninsula. A 'worm' is an old English name for a dragon.

The Dog Who Cries Wolf

What does Queen Victoria have in common with some angry French farmers and a seventies cartoon character? And what does this have to do with the 'montagnes de Pyrenées'? It might not be the shortest way to answer these questions but it's unquestionably one of the most impressive, to drive to the south-west of France...

Whereas the Alps loom, individually superb as you cross the mountainscape, the Pyrenees stretch alongside the route east-west, in their endless borderline, deceptively approachable, impossible to police. Border country; sheep country; wolf - and even bear - country. You catch a whiff of guerilla languages in the place-names, that ripple and hiss, with strange double vowels and text kisses, like Cosledaa or Baudreix.

In the heart of the rich farmland of the Midi-Pyrenées, near the village of Moumoulous, you will find someone extraordinary. Her unassuming manner might fool you but she is unmistakably proud of her 'montagnes'. She will tell you their names, their ancestry back nine generations and when she shows you some of the most beautiful 'montagnes' in the whole of France, you won't be looking south at the grandeur of the peaks but into a nursery rhyme farmyard, complete with free-range chickens, a lame sheep and white dogs the size of bears. For these are the 'montagnes de Pyrenées', the French name for 'Pyrenean Mountain Dogs'. For twenty-three years, Nadine Laffitte has been breeding 'patous', the insider's name for this descendant of Tibetan mastiffs. The dialect word derives from 'pastou', meaning 'shepherd' and in the middle of those flocks speckling the hillsides like pebbles, you will often see a very large shaggy 'sheep' that barks and bites.

Nadine's kennel has witnessed changes over the last ten years and just as the wolf - and now the bear - has been reintroduced to the mountains, so have the angry farmers been turning to traditional methods of protecting their flocks, aided by government grants and education programmes. The patou is not your average sheepdog. It is no traffic policeman and is unlikely to star in 'One Man and His Dog'. It will not race round like a spinning top collecting strays and nipping their ankles. What it does best is lie outdoors. Not bad for a day's work, you might think.

The job requires a dominant position, within sight of your sheep - or of course your humans, if you are one of those patous who has ended up as a family pet. If there is any hint of danger, a wolf, a cyclist or a menacing butterfly, you will bark a warning with your deep voice that can be heard ten fields away - or ten streets. Every good patou knows that the worst dangers stalk at night, so this is when your bark is on a hair-trigger; not a mouse or a noisy neighbour will escape comment. If it comes to it, you will protect your flock to the death. In the past, patous wore spiked collars just in case a wolf put them to the proof - and to keep them awake.

It is hard to believe that these same cuddly teddy bears milling around Nadine's barn can be so fearsome. There is not one growl as the pack welcomes us into its territory - but then Nadine is there. She tells us that puppies from the same de Néouvielle litter are just as likely to be winning prizes at Crufts as working the mountains. Her collection of photographs includes Noustamic winning the Boston Championship. Apparently, the tricky bit wasn't the travel from Moumoulous to Boston but rather getting two patous up an airport escalator.

The popularity of patous as family dogs is etched in media mythology as deeply as Lassie's. Just mention 'Belle and Sebastien' and watch the nostalgia kick in from two generations, whether from the 60's black and white series that crossed the Channel to the U.K. or the 70s cartoon version, which led to a whole new generation dreaming, like me, of a great white best friend.

Whether or not you dream of real fur, if you are tempted to bring back a souvenir next time you visit the Pyrenees, you will be following in the steps of no less a patou-owner than Queen Victoria, whose pet Cabas was the first registered Pyrenean in England. The best time to go is in September, to Argeles-Gazost, where you will find the biggest teddy bears' picnic in the world, at the Annual Special Pyrenean Breeds Show. Ask for Nadine and anyone will point her out to you, discussing canine

27

births, deaths and marriages, amid four hundred dogs in the southern sun. Just bear in mind that you can take the 'montagne' out of the Pyrenees but you can't take the Pyrenees out of the 'montagne'; this will always be a mountain dog and you will always be his sheep...

*montagnes de Pyrenées has the double meaning in French of the Pyrenees mountains and the Great Pyrenees/Pyrenean Mountain Dog
*'One Man and his Dog' is a British TV programme showing competitive sheepdog trials

Spell for Moving House

Widdershins go round and round
weave the spell of places found.

By this rusty tin and lid
cast out all that others did,

cast out spirits long since dead,
dig them deep some earthly bed

far from haunts of humankind,
far from shadows in my mind.

Rose's petal, blade of grass,
stinging nettle, all must pass,

claimed by weather, wind and time,
one in nature and in rhyme.

Come then wind and claim your right
whirl my symbols through the night.

Rose's petal, blade of grass,
stinging nettle - plumb crevasse

and scale the skies, skim the seas,
volcanoes boil and oceans freeze.

Whirl your vortex round the world
and back to tease my fringe uncurled.

My eye of storm is here. Now stay!
Protect my home, my rest, my play.

*Widdershins is an old pre-clock word for anticlockwise commonly
found in occult language*

Mary, Queen of Scots

Child bride, highly strung;
tiptoes crowned, hands wrung.

Husband dead, Scotland calls;
whispered insults, freezing halls.

Calvin's land, pure, proud;
John Knox rants loud.

Pride's fall, sharp blade
spots blood, rapes maid.

White lace, white throat,
black dress (harsh note).

Doe eyes, don's brain,
poet-queen's pulse refrain.

French rhymes, French heart
of Scots line; Scots tart.

Live Safe

I recommend the eight-fold path;

Nourishing diet
Outdoor exercise
Temperate monogamy
Alternative company
Low alcohol
Interesting hobbies
Viable assets
Early nights

May your heart cease to know
the beat of risk.
May your heart not cease.

Not for you
the blind alley on a dark night,
wolf-lope pacing you step for step
as shadows flare on the walls.

Not for you
the huddling in cardboard
or dancing in subways
a tunnel-blown leaf.

Not for you
life's maelstrom nor
the tiger's print in snow.

You Don't Bring Me Flowers

I burned my hand on your thigh
white-hot the air charged with what
we had not done. You stopped the car.
Went shopping while I sat.
Returned
and placed the daffodils you bought
your wife between us.

The Mating Behaviour of Human Beings

Puzzled by her hedgehog spikes,
his paws uncurled her
to her softest.

The Interview

You know that the next time the footsteps echo in the corridor, they will be coming for you. The shiny metal handle will turn, drop like a guillotine. Your turn. The one before you will return, all grimace and sweat, the smell of aftermath.

You re-cross your legs, shifting your buttocks on the hard, plastic seat, finding no other response to the nervous jokes flying across the room, this limbo sized six people by seven chairs and one desk. There will be seven people, temporarily, before it's your turn.

Somewhere, another door opens and shuts. Four shining black shoes tac-tac louder along the corridor, for this is a suits-and-shiny-shoes day. My steps have sounded a wrong note all day, the only heels that clickety-click instead of tac-tac. The only shiny cream shoes, a lacy pattern on the toe. Below the only skirt.

Voices now, professional laughter. 'Ho, ho, ho, it's over. Ho, ho, ho, it's over,' is the real meaning, whatever the actual words before that handle turns. I will go through this door - and through the ceiling I cannot see. I will ignore my bladder and bowels as they are liars. They have had all the attention they need. I will walk, accompanied, to the next door, which will open to me. There will be a Last Supperful of faces turned to me, fixed in the expressions they consider appropriate for the occasion. I will smile, but not too much, will make eye contact, imagine each of them naked on the toilet. I will not imagine this for too long.

The handle turns. The one before me waits politely for me to stand, leave room for him to dive into his chair, leave the room. I do not have time to listen to how it was for him, to benefit from forewarning or fall into the competition's traps.

'Mrs Gill?' I am summoned. I walk through the door. I can do this.

Refined to Bone

Mirror mirror on the wall
I want my body curves
refined to bone.
A little more discipline
more fruit, less fat
will make me all
I ever wanted.
Six stone and losing.
Still too fleshy, slack.
Protruding organs spoil the line
like bra straps, ugly
through a cotton top.
Five stone, ten.
At certain angles I can like myself
but turn this way and still
I see the pulse corrupt the skin,
the swollen shape of womb.
My monthlies stopped three pounds ago.
Five stone, three.
These doctors cannot keep me
from my target. Nearly there.
Only you I trust, my
mirror mirror on the wall.
You'll see me pure
refined to bone.

Going to the Dogs

The mirror had always been an untrustworthy friend, the kind who said 'You look good in pink' but sniggered behind your back. Debra looked at her fifty-four year old self and missed the days when the mirror sniggered *behind* her back. Now the contempt was in the open; her face was a ploughed field, furrows drooping her expression into grim, muddy trenches; her hair was lank swathes of grey, thin on top and trailing its thirty year old style into rats' tails with split ends below her shoulders; her red-rimmed eyes had been a watery, dim brown even before they filled with self-pity; and the contents of her loose polyester top were rolling towards the bulges in her trousers in the anonymous movement of bagged vegetables. Once, she could walk into a room, her feet and head light as dancing, and time made a hiccup for her entry, a heart-stop when the right eyes would find her across the room, and the wrong eyes would notice, then look away. It had been the longest time since the right eyes found her, since her own had dimmed with the hamster-wheel of day-to-day, the deaths and dusting, leaving her alone. Magic? There was no magic. 'You,' her reflection told her, 'are going to the dogs.'

A whine, and a paw scraping her calf demanded her attention because, she corrected herself, she was not alone at all. 'You started life with more wrinkles than I have now,' Debra told the dog sitting beside her. Encouraged, the pug stood on her back legs, scrabbling at her mistress' trousers, whining and beseeching, the deep folds of furry skin making her face look like an aerial view of the Rockies, black lakes for ears, chin and eyes. 'That's enough, Chuckie.' Debra's hand caressed the taupe fur, soft as moleskin. She stared out the woman in the mirror, the only other person she saw these days, apart from the business of living, the necessary check-out assistants, bus drivers and workmen. This was certainly the only other person with whom she was intimate. She shook herself. This wasn't another person. She smiled ironically. And it certainly wasn't someone she liked. She stroked the little dog again, Chuckie's fur was warm and comforting against her hand. 'You wouldn't notice a few more wrinkles, would you, pet. I wish you'd take all of mine.' Debra's skin tightened and tingled, probably some bloody allergy she was going down with. She sighed and went to clean the kitchen. That was as exciting as the day got.

For several days, Debra avoided the mirror. It did her no good brooding over what she'd lost. Far better to take Chuckie to the park and play ball with the one friend who could be trusted. No moods, no lies, no walls of silence. Debra had finished with all that. She'd gone back again and again, offering a fresh start, remembering only what was good, opening that place deep deep inside herself to whatever life brought her. And it had been the same every time; twin thoughts and roses, followed by misunderstandings and barbs, and then the wall of silence. Distance or death, it was all the same. Debra threw the ball for the umpteenth time, knowing that Chuckie would always come back, wagging her tail, panting with the rightness of her world. Until the umpteenth and first time, when Chuckie disappeared behind a clump of rhododendrons and no matter how often Debra called, no Chuckie.

Irritated, Debra marched into the shrubbery to find her dog whining and sniffing bottoms with a sad quivering scrap of a mongrel. All was clearly not right with his world. He was tied to the leg of a park bench with a rope long enough to allow him to crawl into the shrubbery and hide. Half-starved and greasy, his eyes bloodshot, he stared at Debra without malice, waiting for a kick. She should take him to the RSPCA but it didn't take a genius to guess that he'd been abandoned and that no owner was going to show up, tearfully happy at being re-united with their Bonzo or Rex. Instead, she took him home and Chuckie expressed her approval by wagging her tail and peeing in the house.

Bathing the new dog was mostly a question of transferring dirt from the animal to the bathroom walls but there was an unexpected reward. Cleaned up, and after a week of being fed a teaspoon of fish oil with his biscuits, Barnaby, as he was now called, had the rich russet coat of a setter, long and silky. Strands of Debra's own grey hair mingled with Barnaby's rich red as she cuddled him. 'You wouldn't notice a few grey hairs among all of this,' she told him. 'I wish you had mine and I had silky red hair like yours.' Debra sighed and scratched her suddenly itchy scalp, then got on

37

with the chores.

It took most of her time to care for the dogs and carry on with the basics in her own life, so Debra didn't feel the pull of the mirror as much as she had when she'd first stopped looking in it. She thought it was probably better if she didn't think about how she looked at all. After all, the dogs didn't care. So she threw on some old clothes and gathered her hair into a ponytail. Strands seemed to get in her eyes all the time these days so she'd taken to wearing her hair up. Although she barely showed the brush to her own hair, she spent hours grooming the dogs for the sheer pleasure of bringing a gleam to their coat and their eyes. Sometimes, she thought she could feel purring under the hypnotic motion of the bristles along the lie of the fur. Wool-gathering, in the to and fro of the brush and the half-closed eyes of Barnaby, Debra jumped at the sudden stab of pain, confused. Her hand on the brush was still, with its cargo of russet hair, but when she tried to carry on grooming, it was her own hair that was being yanked. Stupid woman! The elastic band had loosened, letting her hair down, sneaking under the brush while she was day-dreaming. She untangled the shiny red hairs, freeing her own, and she finished grooming both dogs.

Something nagged at her as being odd but she couldn't think what. It was at three in the morning when the answers to crosswords and the universe generally arrive, that it dawned on her. However, she knew that 3 a.m. revelations were often daytime idiocies so she turned over and went back to sleep.

Toast, marmalade, coffee and dog-walking all required her early morning body but not her brain and it was nearly lunchtime when she remembered the wrongness. How come there had been no grey hairs? She let down her hair and squinted at it to the left and to the right. It had grown. Obviously it had grown! But should it have grown that much? And as far as she could tell from such a weird angle it looked glossy. And, unequivocally, red. How could she not have noticed? Of course, she had been trying hard not to notice. Inevitably, her train of thought took her to her old, recently neglected friend.

Except that the woman in the mirror was a stranger. Abundant, rich red hair gleaming with amber highlights, clearly in need of brushing, but still. And smooth, clear skin, not one wrinkle on a flawless face. The eyes gave her away though. The woman in the mirror was in shock. Watery brown eyes opened wide and met her own, unmistakably their reflection. Debra looked down below the neck of the amazing woman and saw the same old lumpy body in shapeless clothing. A whine and a paw reminded her of Chuckie and she stroked her absently, then with sudden attention to the wrinkles in the cute folds of the dog's head. Were there more wrinkles than before? She sighed again. How could anyone tell if there were more wrinkles on a pug or a few grey hairs in a red setter's coat. There was only one way to check this out. She looked again at the mirror, assessing the woman coldly. She looked at the two dogs and shook her head. No, they wouldn't do.

For the next week, Debra visited the local animal shelters, explaining that she was looking for a dog, a special dog. As soon as it was clear how choosy she was, the welcome smiles faded and she realized that this wasn't going to work. She turned instead to the local newspapers, feverishly scanning the 'Pets: dogs' column until, after a couple of anxious weeks, she found what she was looking for: '2 year old female husky needs good home due to owners moving house.'

Debra passed the owners' interrogation with honours and the husky passed hers; feisty, not used to children (who cared), good with other dogs (phew) and with the beautiful blue eyes typical of the breed. After appropriate tears (from the ex-owners) and warm enthusiasm (from everyone, including Wolf, the dog) Debra was walking her very own husky back down the street. She was sizzling with anticipation but she would wait until the next day for her experiment, allow Wolf the night to settle into her new home.

Dog-walking with three was an exercise in lead-dancing. Debra clung on until she reached the park, where she unleashed them, relying on Wolf to copy the others in coming when called. Finally, back home, in front of the mirror, she called Wolf to her side and stroked the beautiful cream and grey fur. 'What beautiful blue eyes you have,' she crooned. 'I wish I had eyes like yours.' The mirror wavered in front of her eyes as they watered worse than ever. She swore and fetched a hanky out of the drawer, wiping her eyes clear until gradually she was looking straight into the dim brown eyes of a beautiful young husky, who looked back at her with all of the trust his species generally gives ours.

Debra rushed to the mirror. Blue eyes sparkled back at her, dramatic in that pale, smooth skin against the red hair. But it was a pity that the mouth was so thin and turned down, and that body looked so out of place, like in one of those children's books where you could fit different heads with different bodies. Now, there was an idea. At that moment, the doorbell rang. Nobody ever called unless Debra had summoned them to mend a tap or deliver a pizza, so she checked the spyhole. Only the Postie, with a parcel that wouldn't fit through the letter-box; probably the dog accessories Debra had ordered. She opened the door, took the parcel and growled at the man, who paled and left quickly. Debra turned to the rest of the pack, rubbed against them and went to get scissors to unpack the bedding and treats, new collars and squeaky toys. She stroked the base of her spine absently, where it had been knobbly and irritating all day.

******

The RSPCA Officer hesitated over the telephone but there were so many dogs looking for homes and not everyone could provide for a dog as big as this. He remembered the woman as a little strange but then, who was he to judge? So many people who were good with animals seemed a little strange with humans. Why, his wife had said to him just yesterday that he cared more for his sodding dog than he did for her. Perhaps he shouldn't have told her why that was but what did she expect him to say! So if someone was a bit strange, it didn't mean she'd be no good as a dog owner and that's all he was interested in. Seeing as a husky had been brought into the shelter, and the woman had been so insistent about wanting one, with the usual blue eyes, he ought to follow up the chance of finding a home. He dialed the number but there was no response. He glanced at the address and noted that it was on his way home. He could drop in and that would put his mind at rest too, let him see where the dog was going.

Jim parked the little van he used for work and checked the address. Yes, that was it all right, a typical shabby semi with an overgrown front garden. As he walked up the path, he could hear the barking indoors and when he rang the bell, the clamour was deafening. He waited and the barking started to die down but nobody came to the door. He had been in this job long enough to see all sorts. Some of his workmates said he spoke dog and it was true that he just knew when there was something wrong, however plausible the owner might be. Behind respectable facades, he'd uncovered puppy farms and hidden iguanas, starving donkeys and colonies of caged cats. There was something wrong - he just knew. He tried the door handle and it gave way. Well aware of the dangers of dogs defending their territory, he phoned for back-up. Perhaps the woman had collapsed and needed medical attention. If she returned and he'd called out the boys for nothing, no harm done that a few apologies wouldn't put right. He went back to the van, put on his padded jacket and gloves, got the dog-catcher noose and a crate, and waited.

The moment his mate arrived, Jim nodded to him and opened the door. They were greeted by seven, eight - no, nine - dogs of all shapes and sizes. They looked to be in reasonable condition but their desperation to see Jim made him suspect they'd passed on a meal or two. Jim called round the house and checked the rooms, accompanied by a surprisingly docile pack, but there was no sign of the human occupant. He went into the kitchens where eight empty dog bowls were laid out on the table and he hunted around till he found the dog food. He shared it out, adding a cereal bowl to feed the ninth dog. He was surprised at how well cared for they were and how accepting of his presence. Well socialized, then, and quite clear on who was the leader. Jim observed them as they wolfed down their meal: a cross-breed with reddish coat, a pug, a greyhound running to rolls of fat, a papillon with a sloppy almost human mouth, a clumsy Afghan hound, something that looked like a poodle but with straight hair, a German Shepherd with bad teeth, a brown-eyed husky type - so she hadn't found exactly what she was looking for - and one other.

'That's the leader of the pack.' Jim pointed her out. She had a beautiful curly red coat and tail, neat mouth with bright teeth, blue sparkling eyes and a perfectly proportioned slim body. Even eating, she moved with infinite grace, not gobbling her food like the others. She glanced at him sideways, almost as if she recognized him. Jim shook his head. His wife was right. Work with animals too long and it did things to your head.

'Nightmare!' he shook his head. 'We're going to have to take these back to the shelter and if the owner doesn't turn up that's nine mouths to feed and home. Start with this one. He swung his noose and lassooed the curly red-head, ignoring her snapping complaints as they manoeuvred her out of the kitchen door, into a crate on the lawn and then into the big van. The others came quietly after that.

'Do you think the owner will turn up?'

'Who knows,' replied Jim, closing the van doors.

Some Words to the Moon

Moon
when evening drinks at navy pools
and lays you in the grass,
what troubles you? What hidden urge
disturbs your cool view?

I've seen the billy goat, the buck
and his willing, rolling goat
mate in the bright night, waking heaven
with their noisy … act.

It's like seeing Daphnis
reach his ready Chloe,
nothing in his way.
It's the smell of love
that shakes the moon.

Translated from 'Paroles à la Lune' by Anna de Noailles

Divided by a Common Language

Blog Sept 2013

I t's not news that American English is different from British (my) English. The quotation-title above is attributed in different forms to three different (not American) sources, including George Bernard Shaw and Oscar Wilde, but the observation was definitely expressed at least a hundred years ago and has been repeated many times since. I used to have fun analysing the differences when I was a teacher. I still have fun with some of the misunderstandings. I do not have fun with the consequences for me as a writer.

So let's start with the fun. I mix online with international communities in three virtual worlds; writing, photography and dogs. I'm British and live in France so have made more than my share of mistakes in my second language. Bemused French friends have wondered whether I was really on heat in Vaison-la-Romaine, or why I groom my dogs with a nightie, as I have apparently told them. I love the way my Spanish photographer friends adjust the studio 'lightning' and it explains how they produce such dramatic images. But when it comes to misunderstandings, you can't beat a conversation involving British and American English because each party knows he is right. Forgive me, Australians, South Africans, Irish and all the other speakers of an English which has evolved away from British English for not mentioning you too; I suspect you are still closer to this than to American but I stand to be corrected. After all, The Oxford English Dictionary refers to 'World English' as an alternative.

In one of my online worlds, stock photos, there are strict guidelines about child photography and one of my friends was incensed about the rejection of an image for displaying a two year old child's 'nipples'. The toddler was running around a beach in a happy 'summer ambience' shot and the very idea of such a photo being seen as sexual offended most of us, from most cultures. I find the Europeans more relaxed generally about nudity than the Americans but all of us, from a wide variety of countries and backgrounds, found this photo an innocent image of childhood in summer. One American photographer suggested Photoshopping pasties over the offending nipples.

I didn't like to say but this struck me as a bizarre food fetish. I mean, why would anyone put Cornish meat pies over a child's chest? Or over an adult's nipples for that matter? Curiosity got the better of me and I delicately enquired about the ways in which pasties would enhance the image, along the lines of, 'Wouldn't meat pies look weird on a toddler's chest?' (My time in Yorkshire has given me the delicacy for which that area is famous).

Much laughter later, all the other speakers of proper English owned up that they'd thought the same as I did, all the second-language speakers kept very quiet, and all the American speakers explained that pasties (pronounced differently) are tassels worn by strippers. 'The comment was sarcastic, Jean.' Doh (a useful Americanism).

Not only can words be enemies. Standard American grammar uses 'gotten', which was sent to America on the Mayflower and not used in Britain after that. There is an idiosyncratic use of the conditional tense 'I would have' as past tense, which really grates on me - and these are standard 'correct' usage in American, not slang, so my 'correct' English must grate on Americans. Punctuation conventions also differ; one example is that single inverted commas are the modern norm for dialogue in British English whereas only double are correct in American. Spelling differences are the least of your publication wrongs if you publish the same book in .com and .co.uk online bookshops.

All of this I can accept. Languages evolve and adapt, are rich and changing. What I find irritating is the criticism 'too British' from a few American readers, in reviews of books set in Britain, by British authors (not of mine, so far, but I won't be surprised if it happens). Grammar, spelling and punctuation are criticised when in fact they are correct for British English. I am so grateful for all my many American readers who are aware that these differences exist and are indeed to be expected when you live dangerously and read books in the original English.

Publishers have known all this for donkeys' years and usually have re-writes to suit the market. I suspect that my translation 'Gentle Dog Training' loses American readers the moment they see the words 'lead' and 'lunge' rather than 'leash' and 'longline' but I am incapable of writing in American. If you self-publish you should be aware of the differences when choosing an Editor and when publishing. You can publish and be damned, taking whatever criticism comes, or you can 'translate' your work. Joanne Harris (or her publisher) dumbed down the title of her novel 'Peaches for Monsieur le Curé' for the American version ('Peaches for Father Francis'), wrongly I think.

Of course it would be just as irritating to find reviews on .co.uk criticising American authors for poor English, when they are using standard American, but you know what? I haven't found any yet. Perhaps we're not so insular after all, at least when it comes to forms of English. When it comes to foreign translations, however, there's a very different story to tell...

Haiku from an Ostrich, in Time of War

Tanks roll in hot sand:
planes sing vibrations above:
what a sunny day!

Two Scenes from the Bayeux Tapestry

Fyrdman at Harold's Coronation 1066

(when Halley's comet made an appearance)

Yes, I was there, a fighting man by force,
to pay the dues my village owed the regal axe.
Witan-chosen, bishop-crowned, King Harold
looked the part for thirty heartbeats.

I cheered with the others and I ducked
the hairy star, amazed. Its tail waked fear.
I saw the sparks' reflected curse in Harold's eyes.
Those who fly with him will dive with him;
I'll keep to the rear.

*A fyrdman was a peasant soldier in Anglo-Saxon England, usually
conscripted to pay land dues or as part of his feudal duties to his lord.
*The Witan was the Anglo-Saxon King's Council.
*The Bayeux Tapestry shows 'the hairy star' of ill omen at Harold's
coronation.*

William's Herald: 13th October, 1066

If you look close you'll see me
sitting in the bows of William's ship
in all the usual colours - terracotta, buff and green
in crewels - laid-work on a linen background.
Saxon conscripts in an English workshop
paid this tribute to Bayeux and Bishop Odo -
there he is so upright as he prays and praises
righteous war. The Pope himself has blessed
the bloodshed Harold's broken oath has earned
and with his consecrated banner
sent St Peter's hair as sacred token.
Other lads pass on my words, each to the next;
'Drop anchor; wait until you see light raised
on Mora's mast.' Too quick across,
uncertain landing holds our ships mid-sea.
My trumpet caught their ears and now
they call my message ship to ship.
I fancy as words travel our Duke William's
named The Bastard as at home
and named again from mouth to mouth
for what we hope - that William conquers.

*William's nickname in Normandy was 'the Bastard' then he won the
Battle of Hastings, became King of England and was known from then
on as 'the Conqueror'.*

To an Editor

The 'one word too often profaned'
is apparently 'cat'.
Too many women write too many poems
about, explicitly, 'that'
so I'll try not to write
any poems that bite, that hiss
or that land on their feet.
I'll try to be wary
of words that sound hairy or piss
when they ought to look sweet.
If feline is out, perhaps canine will do
or vulpine, bovine, asinine …
please advise.

I Hope You Like It

If this were a movie premiere
I'd swank in whale-boned strapless gown and emeralds
oozing all the sex-appeal that stardom gives.

Instead I'm here in quiet clothes with well-brushed hair
to hear my poems read by household names.
The hallful shuffle hushes, fills with words I wrote,
my premiere.

Jailbait

On Monday before Maths, Chloe asked me how far I'd gone in the five Fs. I gave the knowing smile I've been practising in the mirror and said, 'What's it to you?' then I turned my back on her but I don't think she was fooled. I could feel her eyes drilling through my sweatshirt the whole time Mr Phillips blah-blahed about probability and exams. Fifteen must be the worst year of your life. I hope so, anyway. Fifteen, the sixth F.

As soon as I got home, I googled to find out what Chloe was on about. The five Fs of life: 'Faith, Fitness, Family, Friends and Finance' didn't sound like Chloe. Nor did the five Fs of fatherhood. As always, you could rely on Facebook: 'Found, Felt, Fingered, Fucked, Forgotten'. Good question, Chloe. How far have I got?

My friend Sue went all the way at Christmas and got pregnant. We skipped Games to talk about it and she told me what colour eyes and hair the baby was going to have. She told me sex made you feel closer to another human being than anything else in the world. So I guess she reached the fourth F. Then she wasn't in class one day and I saw her with her parents, coming out of the Head's Office. She was crying and never looked at anything, as if she couldn't see.

She was back in school a week later, pale and quiet. She avoided me. I wasn't the only one who knew or guessed. All us girls know that the

Head's keen on abortion. Dead keen. I don't see what it has to do with her anyway - it's not as if it happened in a classroom, or even at break - but the parents seem to think her opinion matters. Perhaps Sue is on the fifth F now. She talks to other people but not to me. I suppose I know too much. Maybe she sees the colour of a baby's hair or eyes when she looks at me. I'm never going to have an abortion and no-one can make me.

Last night, I couldn't sleep. I put my pillow between my thighs and squeezed. I imagined it was a man. Not a boy, a man. I don't like boys in that way. They snigger at sex words and they don't live in their own bodies, as if their legs, arms and other bits act without them having any control. Are there five different Fs for boys? Does it have to be five so you can count them on your fingers? Do they only apply to girls so dumb they have to count on their fingers? Not to girls in the top set for Maths with Mr Phillips. He's a real man.

So how far have I got? The usual collection of kiss dares and beery fumbles at parties. When I say I don't like boys, I know what I'm talking about. And Chloe says boys brag. Some of my friends are waiting till they're sixteen but that seems a bit chicken. A boy writes in your birthday card,

'When cherries are red, they're ready for plucking

When girls are sixteen, they're ready for f******.'

And then he gives you an f and six stars in an alley. That's not what I want. I don't want to wait, I don't want a boy and I don't want any Fs. I want to make it different.

It's Monday again, the same lesson that Chloe annoyed me in last week. Symmetry, I tell myself. I'm going to do Maths A level. I take my book up to the teacher's desk while everyone is working on a problem. He should be proud of me. I look him over, calculating the probability, down to the last decimal place. He smiles at me.

Mr Phillips says, 'What can I do for you, Janine?'

Between Wanting and Getting

HUNGER
BEG
STEAL

WANT
?
GET

WIN
ACHIEVE
WORK
WAIT

The Photograph

I thought I'd seen every over-decorated room in the house but no, there was always one more. 'This way,' I was told. Hiding a yawn, I followed the owner into the conservatory, which piled chintz on wicker in a maze of small tables. A ray of sunlight forced entry through the Venetian blinds, dancing on a woman's smile behind glass, a brown-eyed gaze that passed directly to my gut, or lower. She'd hit that sweet spot at the back of the lens, reaching the photographer, reaching me. That's the real professional secret but people don't believe me, even if I tell them. Beauty is indeed in the way you look.

'That's my late wife.' He took the photo back from me, his tapered fingers stroking a curlicue at the edge of the gilded frame. Frowning with what could have been concentration, he replaced the portrait on what a thin line of dust revealed to be the exact spot that it had previously occupied. 'Looking as if she were alive,' he murmured, his fingertip, delicate, tracing the woman's throat from the jut of her chin down to shadowed curves.

'The sittings took an age but that's why you pay a top photographer, isn't it. Not to make her smile, the way only she smiled.' He nodded at me, complicit. 'I saw you notice. Everyone does. Everyone did. There was no need to 'make' her smile - she smiled at every puppy, every 'Have a good day' from strangers, every clichéd compliment. If Drandle - yes, I see you know the artist by name - if Drandle said the light on her hair was pretty or green suited her eyes, that would do it. She smiled at me too, the same smile. No moderation, no distinguishing between what I gave her - a name nine centuries old! - and their daily trivia.'

'It wouldn't do, you know.' His finger tapped the glass, hard, once. 'Then she stopped smiling.' He shook himself out of the reverie. 'Enough about the Drandle. You must see the garden and gazebo; designed by Harbisher himself, perfect background. I'm glad you like the house. My fiancée told me you'd be the ideal wedding photographer. I think you'll do nicely. You're no Drandle.'

Based on the poem 'My Last Duchess' by Robert Browning

Struck Down, in Anger, Ward 39

i) The Test

I have
told them my name,
the month, the year, the season;
listened to the words 'table' 'apple' 'dog';
subtracted sevens from a hundred
till they grew bored at sixty-five;
spelled 'world' backwards
(these last two I'd have failed
before the stroke);
looked at a fixed spot on a spotless wall;
stood, one foot placed behind the other
(but not for long);
boiled a kettle,
poured the water in a teapot;
baked a cake
(I asked the old hands - those who can speak -
'Does it have to rise well?'
They don't know - they're still here).
I remembered 'table' 'apple' 'dog'
to say like some mad mantra.
Now let me out the God-damned hospital -
please.

ii) One Step at a Time

I had to do the stairs twice.
Yesterday I took one step at a time, stopped on all fourteen.
We've only nine at home, then two and two.
The practice stairs are bare. Ours are fewer
and they're carpeted - it's not fair really -
but today I did them all, no problem.
Next step please.
Now can I go home?

iii) Today's Thursday

The doctor only comes on Mondays.

Someone said she'd come today.
I should've asked the staff.
Only doctors sign them,
the release forms.

iv) Friday, 5 p.m.

I love registrars.
Home.

v) At a (Second) Stroke

The hospital has shown its love in four apostles hung above
my bed
in aspects of the human state to help the nurses move my weight
until I'm dead.

Left side, right side, supine, prone
Bless this bed that I lie on.
If I should die before I wake …

Home for good.

Welsh Love Spoon

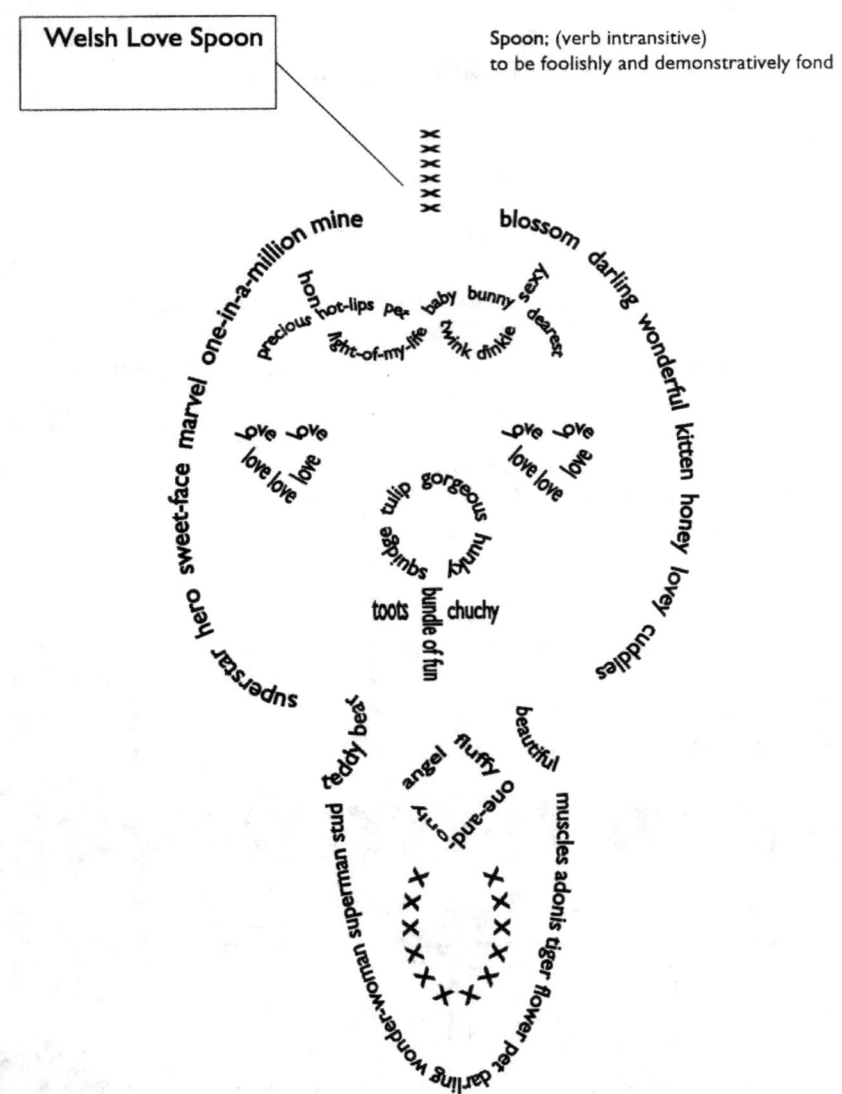

Welsh love spoons were traditionally carved in wood with symbolic cut-outs, and presented as a romantic gift

The True Story of Lou

He had me at 'Ruff!' Internet Dog-Dating

Blog April 2013

The 'Ruff!' part is poetic license as Balou hasn't actually barked in my hearing yet so I don't know what he sounds like - no doubt only one of the surprises in store now that we've adopted a dog. It happened like this...

I ~~read obsessively~~ keep an eye on the French Forum for the Adoption of Big Dogs, telling myself I might be able to offer helpful advice or connect people, that I'm not in any way shopping for a dog, that I'm not a sucker for all those stories of heartbreak and hope. Having worked with a dog trainer (Michel Hasbrouck) I know the dangers of pity, of seeking sainthood via pooches, of bringing home a dog riddled with disease, who is raging against the universe, instead of adopting his quiet friend.

Which is why I ~~fell madly in love~~ made a totally rational decision when choosing a companion for my Great Pyrenees, Blanche, for me, and for my Long-Suffering Husband. It's no secret that I've wanted a second dog for some time but L-S.H. liked the advantages of having only one. I miss dog-dog interaction. I miss the games and I even miss dog dialogue: 'It's my couch... no, it's mine... mine... mine...' ending with whoever's bigger/smarter claiming the disputed territory/object.

Finding a dog through a website *is* a form of online dating and is increasingly important in placing shelter animals. Some refuges are internet-savvy, with professional photos of each inmate; others are suspicious of any contact via a computer and usually too busy to answer a telephone. 'Come and see the dog,' is all the answer you get to your questions about background and character.

I was lucky. I was only trying to get more details about Balou, to help find him a home, as I thought he had a cute face. Yes, photos/ appearances make the first impression and some dogs just appeal to you more than others. Separately, two shelter workers gave me more information about Balou, not realising that I was interested for myself (unsurprising, as I didn't realise this either). Both people said that this Briard-cross had 'a character of gold', the French idiom that I would translate as 'a sterling character' (interesting aside on national currencies and character descriptions). In any language, he's considered a cutie-pie. He gets on with people and with other dogs. But the words that etched themselves into my brain were these (I translate):

'He is one of those dogs we nickname 'the invisible ones'. People never notice them. Because he's black? Black is out of fashion and nobody wants a black dog. And yet he has so many great qualities.'

Balou has been in a shelter for two years and not one person has even looked at him. He was abandoned due to divorce. He lost his family, including the children he loved (according to the couple who left him at the shelter). His friend the German Shepherd was abandoned with him but found a home straight away. Balou has lived with different dogs since then; they come, they find a home and they go.

Apparently, L-S.H. was tired of seeing a dog's face on my computer screen every time he looked, so he said, 'Yes'. We went to see Balou on Wednesday, taking Blanche with us so that we could have the first meeting on neutral ground and judge the two dogs' reactions.

We walked them on lead and one training need was clear straight away - Balou pulls like hell. The dogs ignored each other and Balou even ignored another refuge dog playing macho on the opposite side of the road - all good signs from my viewpoint. Then we let the dogs loose in an enclosed area.

Balou wasn't interested in us but that's often the case with shelter dogs, especially with strangers. Part of the training work ahead is for us to form a relationship with an adult dog. However, he was confident with us, didn't mind being stroked, even on his head (a dominant gesture to a dog so should never be the first approach) and his eyes are full of warmth and fun, despite two years in a shelter. The introduction couldn't have gone better and I can't wait for the 6th of May when we can pick up Balou and bring him home. We already had holidays booked and I'd rather he stays in the refuge with people he knows than go to a boarding kennel.

Inevitably there are memories of Bétel, the friend we lost three years ago. Nobody can replace him but there is room in our life and hearts for Balou. It seems fitting that my book 'Someone to Look Up To', with Bétel's beautiful face on the cover, is now in amazon uk's top 100 kindle dog books and I was wondering how Balou would fit into the characters living in the refuge, described in the mid-section of the book. Prince maybe? The five-year old black dog? Or perhaps Sirius himself, in character not in looks, the dog who 'kept the faith.'

Dog Adoption

Blog May 2013

Now I know why experienced dog adopters are reluctant to put in writing their advice beforehand; each dog comes with 'previous', good and bad, which affects his reactions; each adoptive family offers and wants different behaviour from the dog in widely differing family contexts; much of 'what you should do' is in body language, relationships and good timing - so difficult to explain or teach; and most successful dog adopters have absolutely no idea why they're good so they can't explain the skills they've added to instincts from experience. I still think it helps to share what we learn so here's my experience so far.

Yesterday was the day of truth; Day 1 of the rest of his life, chez nous, earlier than planned because the rain just keeps hammering down and we cancelled our holidays. Great! We could get Balou sooner! Note crucial fact already mentioned: the rain keeps hammering down. Lou is not a dog; he is a furry hippo who threw himself into a deep, full mud-hole in our garden and wallowed. He already smelled like two years in a cage, fur like a carpet from a dumpster. I very rarely bath dogs but I decided to make an exception, using the special 'shampooing pour les chiens noirs' that had tempted me with its promise of making black fur blacker and shinier.

Would I advise someone to throw buckets of warm water over the new arrival within hours of starting his new life, followed by a soapy massage, more buckets of water and then a game of chase round the garden with a towel? I don't think so! But it worked for us. While my Great Pyrenees watched the peasants cavorting and stayed well away from the wet stuff. It didn't take a canine genius to figure out that Lou liked water (the dirtier, the better) and I felt confident in handling him because of the car journey.

I haven't told you about the car journey? No problem getting him in the car with a traditional 'run at open back door' method. We waved goodbye to Nice Lady at Shelter, who wants 'after' photos. Then we fought to keep dog from jumping over to join us in the front seat, stopped the car, and re-arranged the people for Plan B. I put a seat up and joined Lou in the back of the Berlingo. An hour's drive later, I knew where he liked being stroked and I smelled like two years in a cage.

I was wrong in thinking it would take time for Lou to take an interest in us. He's lying beside me as I type and, now he's away from the shelter, there's no doubt he wants us to be his people and he wants to be with us - both of us. If he hears a door, he checks out who's coming through it and his tail will need a service from wagging so fast and so often. Change is difficult and tiring, even change for the better, and I know many dogs try to run back to what is familiar, even if the familiar is physical abuse or neglect. There's no sign of Lou trying to do a runner but we're being careful - walks are on-lead.

He loves grass. He rolls in it, chews it, lies on it. The only grass he's seen in two years was a strip where the shelter dogs get walked every three to four days. He hadn't been out of his cage for three days when we picked him up. He loves being brushed, apart from two knotted dreadlocks dangling from his ears. I don't know whether he's been brushed at all in two years (or before that). He lived in an infernal noise at the shelter, amid construction work as well as all the barking, and he seems surprised at Blanche playing guardian to a passing bicycle or the postvan. When she barks, he points, in the classic gundog pose, but so far he hasn't spoken.

Amazingly, his behaviour indoors is civilised - no attempts to steal or destroy - and he is house-trained. When you think about him spending up to four days in a cage without leaving it, what a miracle that he has kept the habits presumably learned with the family of his first five years. That doesn't mean there's been no territory-marking. He's a full-blooded male and when he peed on the veranda door, he was told a clear 'No.' I cleaned it by the book, with white vinegar (never bleach or the smell encourages repeat crimes). He watched, waited and returned to finish the job that I'd interrupted. He obviously hasn't read the same book! Since then he's lifted his leg against another interior door, recollected himself (or decided that I was watching) and refrained. My husband is already referring in franglais to 'the Big, Bad Loup' since we shortened Balou to Lou.

I am exhausted but, so far, this is an easy adoption of a dog who wants to please, who gets on with people and other dogs. However, the Princess already in residence is not an easy dog; she is polite to others (human and canine) but unknown humans should keep their distance and dogs should show respect, especially in doorways. So far, we've passed potential flashpoints without incident: going in the car together, mealtimes, a quiet night (hooray), even doorway negotiations. Sometimes it doesn't matter what decision you, the master, take; what matters is that you do take a decision and give clear signals to the dogs, over matters such as getting in and out of the car. With dogs like Lou, anything goes but not with dogs like Blanche.

They have played chase and fallen asleep together (in a thunderstorm - an unexpected flashpoint!). It's a good start to what I hope will be a great friendship but I'm watching my Great White very carefully - almost as carefully as she's watching me...

My top tips on dog adoption

Tell your dog sweet nothings in a low, purring tone. Tell him when he's doing things right (which includes when he's doing nothing at all). Thank you, Michel Hasbrouck, for this simple but under-used technique.

Secure the perimeter and walk on lead for at least 2 months (and better forever than lose your dog).

Predict the flashpoints, especially if you have another dog, and plan for the practicalities. Anything involving travel, food, close quarters, sleeping arrangements, attention from the master, comings and goings, visitors, could be stressful.

After you've got him home –

4 common stages in dog adoption

1) Just Visiting

The first two months can be honeymoon heaven, with artificially good behaviour because the dog hasn't yet got his paws under the table. Family pets can be over-polite to each other and all the bad habits you allow because you feel sorry for the woes suffered by your dog in the past, can bite you in the butt (literally) when he's settled in. Escape bids are common because the dog is seeking to return to familiar territory.

The beginning of an adoption can also be hell, especially with a dog who's known abuse - and often you don't know the history of your new family member. Be calm and careful with introduction to other animals, other family members. Avoid more flashpoints than are necessary - life will bring more than enough.

Whether heaven, hell or in between (does that mean purgatory?!) this too will pass.

2) Integration
Usually some time in the first two months. Everyone realises that the new dog is here to stay - including the new dog. Everyone tries to figure out how he fits in and where he fits in. Resident dogs stop being polite to the visitor and they have dog-dog sort-outs of the pack hierarchy. One new dog means that every privilege, every toy, every relationship, is up for grabs.

3) Testing
The new dog has his place in his family but he's the sort who wants more. If you've given him everything he wants from the start, and he's been easy-going about it, he might start to cash in on it now, by bullying you. Or he might be a 'benevolent tyrant' who knows he's in charge but doesn't bother acting on that knowledge. If your adopted dog starts pushing you around, you have to stop him, without hitting or shouting.

4) Your dog in his pack
Everyone is happy but...

5) Testing
never stops with some dogs and you go through Steps 3,4, and 5 all of the dog's life. It's how the dog checks you are up to the job of leading, that you are 'Someone to look up to'.

Read Part 2 of Lou's story on page 76.

A Shot in the Dark

Trespass is my territory. I duck under chains, pass the No Access! Danger! and Keep Out! signs, which are all meant for other people. My talisman against harm is in my backpack and my tripod butts me like a friendly dog as I walk the empty streets. Old warehouses creak their wooden whispers in silhouettes. The night cityscape bears no likeness to its daytime self, bled of colours except where neon, street-lamp or moon blast strange shadows.

I pass the blanket-rolled bodies in doorways, their bottles and boots, their brown dogs. I am invisible in my black clothes and beanie hat. Leaves and litter drift towards corner piles, soggy underfoot. The siren-wail stays distant - good. Nearby shouting alerts me. I cross the wasteland to avoid two overcoats with heads, looming into conflict, arms raised and wrestling for a small cuboid. Silver glints enough to maybe show at a high ISO setting. One grunts and falls. They move too fast for a good shot in this light and I'm not interested in people. I lose sight of them. I'm looking for night grunge, the bare bones of a building, leading lines of light. I'll know when I find it.

My camera will capture the scene by the inhuman laws of physics. To take the shot, I must see in long exposure and mixed lighting. What I see as white could be violet, yellow or red to the camera. Which of us is right? What is the relationship between data and interpretation? Between my camera and me? For I am not alone although my companion is an alien, who tempts me to prise off a wooden plank, breaking and entering an abandoned store. Moonlight shafts from window to graffitied wall and I know this is the place.

I set up the demanding overseer on its three legs. I dance torchlight patterns into the basilisk gaze of a wide-angle lens. I make myself disappear, become a no-one in black. Only bright light and static objects exist. A mountain's view of the universe, where human lives flash ephemeral across millennia. My photo will show the torch track as one outlined dragon with real fire at its maw, where I lit the flare. I have dreamed this shot, the dragon hiding in the city, challenging the moon from its urban lair.

Then the sirens get too close for me to ignore. My torchlight and fire have attracted the attention of forces who like the night to be predictable. They see me. But they never see the bodies in doorways nor the others who live in the dark. I am just a visitor and must be punished. I am easier to punish than the others. My exquisite composition is broken by the door (smashed open) and flashlight (blinding and neutral, would need a tungsten gel to balance with the blue of moonlight).

'It's him again, alright.' The officer is backlit with a halo effect on young blonde hair from the flashlight directed badly by his colleague. I want them to change positions to make the most of the height difference but I know better than to say so. And anyway, I'd need to change my settings.

'He must have seen something,' says the shorter one, eyes overshadowed by his cap. The shadows create a threat that compensates for his stature. 'You.' He means me. 'Did you see something going on by the waste-ground?'

'Yes,' I tell him. 'The moon was visible just above the chimney of the old pottery and I could have got a shot that lined up the clock too. I'd like to get the clock in the frame. But I couldn't put my tripod where I needed to. Not tonight.'

Eyes narrowed. 'Why not tonight? What was different?'

'The recycling bins,' I tell him. 'They'd been moved. They were in my way.'

'Leave him, Joe. It's not worth the effort. We've slammed him in the cooler before for breaking and entering but he's always back. We've got a murder to deal with and you know the only thing this loonie will say in his statement.'

They go, with no goodbye. I can't resist a quick preview. There's the dragon, glowing at the heart of the night city. And there's a grab shot I'd forgotten. I zoom and confirm. The silver glinting was a knife. Blood doesn't show red in the dark. Surprisingly sharp really. The shot, I mean. But I'm not interested in people so I delete it, pack up and head for home.

Trespass is my territory.

The Wild Dutch Roo of la Drôme

for Laurent 'the Chameleon' on his 75th birthday
(a Dutch-French-Australian artist living in la Drôme, France)

The Laurent-tides have swept
Seventy-five years of flotsam and jetsam
Since boyhood and Bondi.

The Chameleon has seventy-five spots,
prints on a man's soul, places
shifting with language and light.

The nuggets of thick black paint
On the Saracen tower and the Souspierre cliffs
can never be Dutch-washed.

Lavender blues behind his mother's house
while the robot cleans the swimming pool.
The whiplash snake blesses his atelier

And the cicadas sing the birthday present.
La cigale chante l'anniversaire et l'éphémère.
De cicade zingt het verjaar dags genu schenk.

**Laurent's landscapes include the view from his house of the Saracen
tower and the Souspierre cliffs. The last two lines are an attempt to
translate the last English line into French and then Dutch, choosing
different meanings of the word 'present'.*

Aren't They Sweet Children

You tidy toys
and find White Rabbit
spatchcocked on the dinosaur duvet
(synthetic fur, bead eyes like blood,
pink satin ear-tufts)
and you check the DVD player
wondering
about the innocence of childhood
worrying…
trying not to remember.

Why Did the Little Boy Kiss the Glue?

Queuing in the post office, I saw a toddler
stretch to kiss an ordinary packet, vacuum-wrapped,
neatly hooked at child's eye-height.
In the pack a glue stick, white with lettering.
He pressed his lips in private pact (he thought).
He thought. Then smile-less went about his day.
Why?

Confused?
'I'm hot. I think that shiny ice-cream's cool.
It's not.
How do grown-ups always know
beforehand? I must go.'

Freudian?
'A willie-shape and twinkly bright!
If I had one like that
my Mum just might…
P'raps one day.'

Literary?
In later years he reminisced
'twas artists' thoughts made flesh, he'd kissed,
and oft when crafting abstract works
he'd muse on childhood's visual quirks.

I only know, at thirty-six,
I never should have knelt
to kiss the plastic-packaged glue
and wonder what he felt.

ANGELA 1979

Dogs Digging Each Other

Blog May 2013

After 2 weeks...

Lou, our adopted dog, is still amazing us by how civilised he is, despite more than two years in a cage. He loves knowing what will happen next, whether it's a walk in the woods or bedtime. He loves water on the ground but not from the sky. If he sees a puddle, he lies down in it. Yet his reaction to the hose - recoil - reminded me of his past; shelter cages get sluiced out with hoses. We are lucky with Lou, who is a plucky character, eager to please us and to fit in, but he also has a history that we can only guess at from his behaviour.

Now he is part of our lives, it hurts to imagine what his previous two years were like. He has been fully house-trained here from the moment he arrived (apart from marking his territory a couple of times on the veranda and cellar doors). Imagine how upsetting it must have been for him to foul his cage. Thanks to volunteer dog-walkers he was given 'a walk' every 3 to 4 days. In between, he was waiting for that walk - or trying to wait. The walk itself consisted of five minutes pulling on the lead, five minutes freedom on a strip of enclosed grass where he could run about and relieve himself, then five minutes pulling on the lead, back into the cage. Even after a fortnight, two shampoos (on the first day!), and a few rain-showers, I think I can still smell the cage and I want that smell gone, forever. Every day, more dead fur comes out on the brush. I want his coat gleaming like his eyes.

Lou has other ideas about his coat. Not only is mud good for hair and skin, it is excellent for bonding two dogs who like digging. The relationship between my Great Pyrenees, Blanche, a.k.a. the Princess, and Big Bad Lou, started off politely. The Princess was magnanimous and the Peasant cautious, not least because at 32kg he weighs in at 20kg lighter than she is. Then they started an engineering project in the garden. This involved serious digging. The holes filled with water and the furry hippo immediately sat in one. Who knows what Blanche was really planning for Lou but from the moment they started digging together, they moved closer to friendship.

I think the honeymoon is over and we're into Stage 2. Non-stop rain has both dogs bored and looking for trouble (i.e. each other) so this morning witnessed the first session of full dog-dog physical interaction. Lou's style is kung-fu - in fast, out faster, left-right left-right with the paws, then bounce off the furniture and chew the rug. Blanche has a certain elegance in her approach; the play-bow and a lot of vocalising, but the finish is pure sumo wrestler. She's a heavyweight and believes that jumping on your opponent's stomach usually settles things. Not if he's fast enough. They seemed to be playing to the same rules and tails were wagging throughout so I was more concerned for my living-room than for the dogs but I can appreciate what this stage is like when either dog turns aggressive. Then it's often a return to the shelter for the adopted dog, with bad habits reinforced.

Incidental dog training is all around us and I'm trying not to overload Lou when everything is new but rather to take advantage of opportunities that arise naturally - such as a wine-buying trip. I suspect that Lou's wine knowledge is limited so we took him and Blanche to the May fête day at a Seguret wine cellar, about an hour's drive from here. Dog-wise it was a good test of a long journey, which will be useful for when we all go on holiday in September (if we're still feeling brave); people-wise, it was a good chance to stock up on Côtes du Rhône Villages. 'Nickel! Impecc!' as we say in France when something has gone well. I'd rather Lou didn't pile over into the front seat every time the car stops but that's fixable.

In a formal training session, I have taught him, 'Thou shalt not pull on the lead' so that walks are now a pleasure, if a bit of a tangle with all four of us and two lunges. From now on, he is no longer allowed to pull on any form of lead. Orderly behaviour getting in and out of the car was progressing nicely and then the hydraulics gave out on the back door, so the dogs now have to get in and out of side doors. So much for establishing a routine and keeping to it. Lou's a bright little button and he's adapting;

for a different dog, each change would be a setback.

I wasn't prepared for his silence. Not just the lack of barking (compared with Great Pyrenees who have for years alerted me to every passing fly and cleared the area of wolves in at least a twenty mile radius) but the lack of all sound. Apparently this is common in adopted dogs. Sometimes they bark for the first time months after being in their new home. The noise in an animal shelter is ear-shattering; some dogs join in, some retreat to silence, and many are traumatised. All I know about Lou in kennels is that he was not 'a barker'. In his second week I've heard him growl once, when Blanche thought she'd investigate his food bowl. To me, this is a good sign and Blanche understood exactly what was meant. He has made a little barking noise, twice, so small that I wondered if I'd dreamed it. The first time, he was shut in the garden with my husband and Lou could hear me on the other side of the door. He wanted to come in. I didn't let him because I don't want him calling the shots. The second time was when Blanche pushed him to play. She is very vocal, with a whole range of play vocabulary and it touched me to hear him reply - even if that response was probably, 'Get stuffed, I'm sleeping!' When I hear Lou talking, I'll know he really has his paws under the table.

I do worry about the perception that I'm a nice person because I've adopted a dog - nicer than someone buying a puppy from a responsible breeder. I've done both. Would I adopt another dog in the future? Yes, if it fitted in with what suited our family. Do I think people should adopt dogs, not buy puppies? No, I do not! I think it's a personal choice. I wish there were no dogs in shelters at all and no adoption. When I translated the book 'Gentle Dog Training' it was in the hope that dog-owners would seek help for 'difficult dogs', not abandon them. I wish the only dogs were those brought into the world in, and for, loving families and I completely support responsible breeders. I wouldn't hesitate to support such a breeder by choosing to buy a puppy from her - as I did with Blanche. What matters to me is the commitment to your puppy and to your dog, for life.

Lou won't be going back to the shelter, however much he starts chewing the rug, and Blanche will still be our dog, however much she starts chewing Lou.

The Voice of Dog - Lou Speaks

Blog June 2013

The plumber did it. After three weeks of being almost mute, one sight of the little white van outside our gates was all it took for our adopted dog Lou to join Blanche, our Great Pyrenees, in alerting us to the threat - or workmen, as we call them. The voice is mid-range, a little rusty and hoarse, and music to our ears. It means that Lou knows he's home, not just on holiday. Having found his voice, he showed us the full range when a police siren passed by. Some dogs respond to the siren tone by howling and we now have two of them who throw their heads back and audition for 'The Jungle Book'.

Another sign that Lou is settling in is that he sometimes prefers to lie peacefully in the hall in the evening rather than watch gruesome murders and C.S.I. investigations; each to his own. Choosing his place, distancing himself a little from us now and then shows confidence, and there's no lack of attention to us all day. So where have we got to with our adoption?

Health Costs

It doesn't matter whether a dog is seven years or seven months, the outlay on vet's bills is an expensive lottery. Big dogs cost more and living in a shelter does no favours for a dog's health. So far we've spent 140 euros to get Lou from the shelter; and a further 200 euros on three visits to the vet and medication. The routine medication includes worm tablets, 6 months' flea and tick treatment (our region of France is tick-infested), and a solution for rinsing ears. The non-routine medication has been for an ear infection (complicated by an insect sting) and for a cough.

Neither condition has stopped him bouncing through life like Tigger but I'm hoping to clear up both. It's part of the settling in period to face whatever health problems my new dog brings with him.

The unkindest cut - whether to neuter or not

Most shelters require a new owner to neuter an entire dog as a practical measure to prevent unwanted puppies (likely to become the next generation of inmates). We had Blanche sterilised young, to minimise her risk of mammary cancer and because we didn't want to breed from her. We have a fenced garden and haven't had a problem with dogs escaping so, when the shelter left us the choice, we left Lou's bits entire.

The experts all disagree about neutering male dogs. Vets and many behavioural trainers want male pet dogs neutered; they say it prevents unwanted puppies (true) and unwanted behaviour (debatable). Breeders and some dog-trainers are against neutering male pet dogs unless there are medical grounds; they say neutering can change the dog's character and even induce unwanted behaviour (debatable), and there are other ways of preventing sexual activity. I don't know what's best for other people but I'm happy with full-blooded males, including dogs. I've never had a dog trying to mount the furniture or me (thank God, given that my last male, a Great Pyrenees, weighed 70kg) and I'm convinced that such behaviour is about dominance not about sex, so requires training, not a surgeon's knife. Dogs are not people and if there's no scent of bitch-on-heat, there are no sexual fantasies.

All the experts agree that neutering a female has big health advantages. The disagreements are about when to neuter. Vets advise, 'early'; breeders advise, 'after the first season'. Having made our personal choice with Blanche, which was to trust the vet who would have to perform the surgery, we felt comfortable leaving Lou entire. If we had decided otherwise, or been so compelled by the shelter, we'd have had the complication of convalescence to add to the settling down period of an adopted dog - not something I'd have enjoyed.

I'm lucky in being able to afford the time and the money required. I'm also lucky in that Lou accepts handling from me and from the vet but I have had a dog who wanted to kill vets. He had good reason but that didn't help me at all with 70kg of angry dog and a vet who wanted nothing to do with him - also understandable. What did help me was a) the training I'd done with him since he was a puppy so he was used to me touching him and b) a Shellclip muzzle. So I dealt with it. Better than that, thanks to a co-operative vet, we gradually brought back my dog's willingness to be touched by a stranger.

However, I wonder whether I could handle 70kg of adopted dog, who hadn't known me from puppyhood, who wouldn't let me touch him and who hated vets. There are plenty of such dogs in shelters. If I fell in love with a giant rescue dog who was really difficult to handle, would I cope? Loving giant dogs as I do, this is a consideration if I adopt again in the future. Maybe starting with a puppy would be wiser if I choose a giant breed? Or at least choosing a dog I can literally handle, like Lou in temperament.

In my part of France, vets are not like they were in the UK. The dog's behaviour is my responsibility. If the vet can't get the vaccine up the dog's nose because the mutt is behaving like a kangaroo, I'm given the phial in a little take-away bag to 'do at home when she's calmer'. This involves sneaking up on said mutt when she's asleep and assaulting her like the Pink Panther's manservant, trying to inject her nose. It is not easy! And I miss the Welsh vet, who brought in a vet's nurse and a fellow-vet to assist in pinning my giant dog to the floor while stitches were removed. In Wales, vets' nurses were part of the team. Here, with Blanche, it's just me, the vet and a kangaroo. And while Lou might be perfect during treatment, he has expressed how he really feels by cocking a leg on the way out of the pristine consultation room. Maybe keeping him entire has its drawbacks after all.

'Anyone who stops learning is old, whether at twenty or eighty. Anyone who keeps learning stays young. The greatest thing in life is to keep your mind young.' Henry Ford

This goes for dogs too and you *can* teach an old dog new tricks. Lou is seven years old, has spent the last two years in a shelter cage and he is a great student. Of course it is possible that he was winning Crufts obedience trials in the five years before he was dumped by a divorcing couple but somehow I doubt it. I don't doubt that he *could* win obedience trials with the right training but that's not what I do. In formal training, this is what I do with my dogs:-

The 5 Pillars of Dog Wisdom:-

Leadwork, Recall, Downstay, Turn-taking and Aperitifs

I'm sure that Lou had plenty of people-experience and some training when he lived with his previous family but whatever commands were used were definitely in French. Ex-Balou has switched language as easily as changing his name. He reads body language, listens to the tone of voice and uses his knowledge of how people behave to figure out he's expected to jump in the car, go outside for a pee or come into the house.

From the way he behaves now, my guess is that Lou used to come when called. It's possible that he walked nicely on a lead but if so he lost the habit in the shelter and has now regained it. He was definitely never taught a long downstay but one long, determined (on both our parts!) formal session taught him and he will now lie down for half an hour or more when he is told, where he is told, until he is released from the command. Thank you, Michel Hasbrouck for training me!

These three pillars of training let me take Lou to the market, to friends' houses, for a coffee in the village... in a word, give me freedom. That is the essential paradox of dog-training and of my life too; self-control (the dog's, and mine) gives greater freedom.

You'll have noticed five tenets in the training sub-heading, not just the big three. That's because Lou added two more. Turn-taking was entirely Lou's idea and started with his enthusiasm for doing a 'sit' (something that's fun but not important to me). Once a day, Blanche sits on command, waits and, when given the OK (literally, as that's our release word) chases after a chew treat, then plays cat-and-mouse with it before eating it. I wanted both of them to have their chew treat and Blanche still to have her fun so I just hung on to Lou's collar to stop him going after Blanche's titbit. He didn't just wait patiently; he sat, watched and moved when told 'OK'. So the next day, I told them both to sit - two bums hit the ground. I released Blanche; Lou waited, still sitting. I gave him the OK, throwing his chew at the same time and he was off like a bullet. That is now our routine and I am so proud of him for training me so well.

And then there are the aperitifs. As we live in Provence, we have the ~~daily~~ occasional aperitif. Since Blanche was a puppy, she and her then partner-in-crime were in the habit of rushing to the kitchen on the magic word 'Aperos!' where they received ice cubes from the big American fridge. The first time the call 'Aperos' went out, Lou rushed to the kitchen with Blanche, only to be sadly disappointed at getting an ice cube, which he spat on the floor. However, convinced that anything the big blonde likes must be worth trying, he has now become addicted to crunching up aperos and is first there at the very sound of a Martini being poured. Speaking of which, I think it's time... 'APEROS!'.

Barbarossa, Dirty-Beard

Blog July 2013

All happy dogs have many nicknames and our Big Bad Lou is no exception. I wasn't worried about his ancestry, thinking him to be what a French friend calls 'a Crusader dog' and what we used to call 'Heinz varieties' (from the soup advert offering 57 varieties) but then the same French friend told me that Lou looked very much like the old-fashioned Briard from which he is supposedly a cross-breed. What I found out about the breed fits Lou to an L.

The Briard Breed

Briards are also known as Bouviers de Flandres, Belgian in origin, and were known in more familiar terms as koehond (cow dog), toucheur de boeuf or pic (cattle driver), and - my favourite - vuilbaard (dirty beard), No prizes for guessing the origin of this nickname

83

and because Lou's beard is bleached and aged a reddish-brown, and he has a certain presence, 'Barbarossa' was inevitable. Despite the nicknames, Briards have a noble history: Charlemagne, Napoleon and Thomas Jefferson are among the famous afficionados of the breed.

In both World Wars, Briards were the war dogs used by the French, almost to extinction. They carried messages, searched for wounded soldiers and were commemorated with awards and sculptures (neither of which would have meant as much to them as a game of hide-and-seek with their masters). They are apparently dominant dogs but as my breed of choice for twenty years has been the Great Pyrenees, I wouldn't notice!

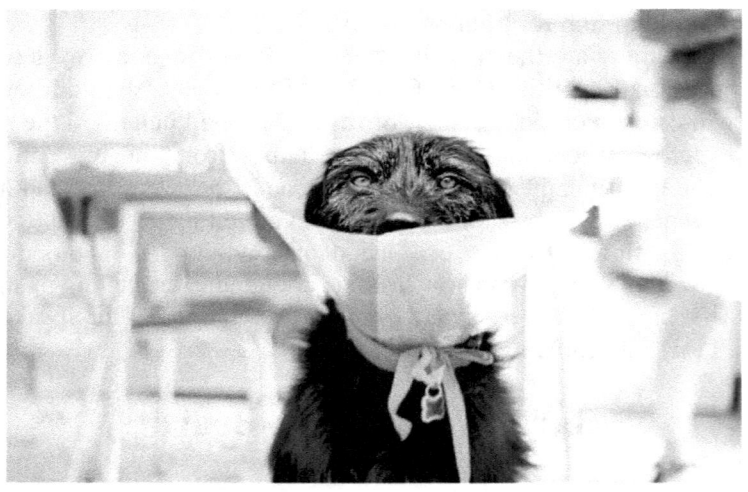

Eye Contact - Good!

Lou seems happy with all his names and his training has progressed so that he now looks me in the eyes, knowing that I want him to. How does he know? Because every time he looks towards me, or actually catches my eye, and I notice, I tell him how beautiful he is. Some trainers believe you should behave like a dog, avoiding eye contact, and they are right that an unknown dog will consider eye contact to be a threat, but my dogs know that I am not a dog. They trust me and it is beautiful when we look into each other's eyes. It is not challenging (although I've had that too, from previous dogs).

I can't yet get this contact on walks as Lou still has what I call crazy-escapee syndrome, even though he doesn't pull now. He does behave as if he's just escaped from the shelter and has to make the most of his five minutes of freedom. So I'm working on this, the same way I've worked on contact in the house and garden - with compliments when his behaviour is closer to what I want.

It's just as well that Lou trusts me as we've visited the vet once a week since he arrived here, sometimes without him lifting a leg on her cabinet but always with his intention to do so. The score so far is Lou 3; Jean 4. Dogs with floppy ears are prone to dirty and infected ears, and although I've cleared up the big infection, Lou still has some dirt deep in the ear canal (according to the vet), and hairy ear interiors, so I'm looking at natural ways of regularly cleansing the ears, without poking objects such as cotton buds into them (too dangerous). At the moment I've settled on olive oil, alternating with vinegar/sterilised water on a separate occasion, injected carefully with a small syringe, massaged and any debris swabbed out with gauze. Once a week with the olive oil, which Lou likes, and once a week with the vinegar mix, which he doesn't mind.

In addition to his ear infection, Lou's had a split callus on his elbow, which was being licked into something nasty. How ironic that after two years on concrete, summer weather on ceramic tiled floors seems to have done the damage. I've seen how quickly skin problems can turn to a putrid nightmare in our summer heat, traumatising dog and owner, but Lou has healed quickly with only natural medication - thank goodness. The side- and long-term effects of Cortizone and antibiotics can be as much of a nightmare as the initial skin problem. Lou did have to wear a collar and he wasn't pleased.

However, the rewards of virtue followed quickly, and we took him and Blanche for a swim in our special place - clean and quiet. I vowed I would get him shiny and I think I'm getting there.

Even a clean river here can spark skin problems so our latest gadget is a solar-heated outdoor shower for summer fun and dog practicalities. Lou is about as keen on water-from-above as he is on wearing a collar but he is a natural in front of the camera so he did a turn while everyone else fooled around with the shower.

He has now started his modelling career for stock photos and is a real star. This was supposed to be 'the training class' but he and Blanche are more interested in each other than in the supposed training - too true to life!

This is already my favourite photo of the summer and friends have suggested I've invented a new sport - water-dog-ski. For me, it's a photo of happiness, of the summer Lou came.

Read Part 3 of Lou's story on page 111.

Springtime

Green branch for the Ferryman or for the dove
that brought peace to the Ark. Ah, the green taste
of bushes clipped by dreaming goats.

To be a goat, untethered, dazzled by the wealth
of gleaming buds, a shining halo
greening over fields - to head straight
among the tinkling bells
into the wandering stream;
to follow each new whim
to skitter sideways only for the dance
to laugh into the wind
for nothing but the laughter… Like Before!

First leaves
little fingers all in shells
children's fingers green with gleaming life
leaning on old walls towards us.
The old wall murmurs, 'Beware the mad wind,
beware the sun's glare and the dazzling night
beware the goat and the caterpillar,
beware life itself, little fingers of green.'

A translation of 'Printemps' by Sabine Sicaud

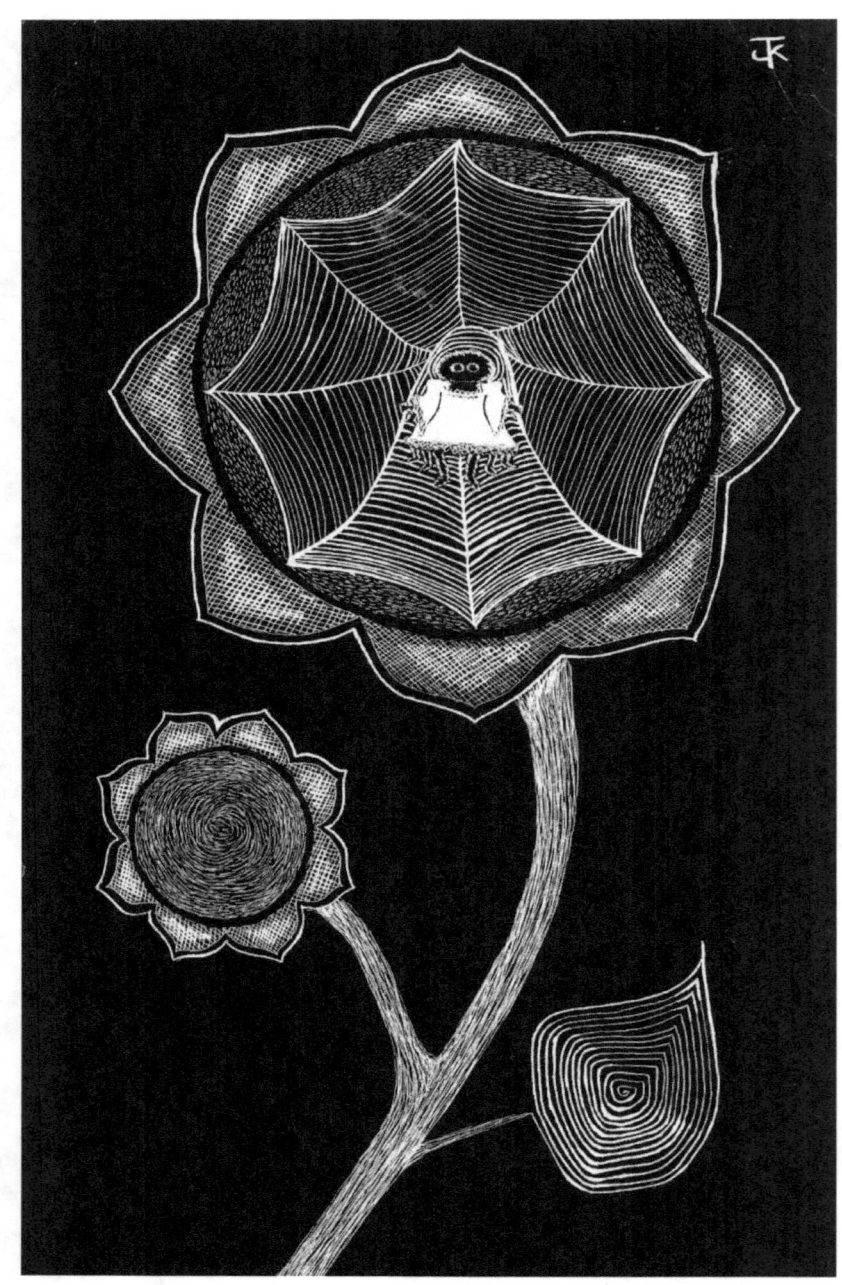

Winter

She said that she had walked for far too long
unbalanced by the weight of words unsaid,
of too much pain.

She said that she could not go on;
the future was just more
of what had gone before,
more pain again.

She said that living on was just too hard -
she'd lost all faith in sunshine
and the silent depths of churches,
flinching at each smile of mine,
ice to her core, wintered too sore.

Never wind colder,
never rain wilder
than the night - her twentieth -
when she stilled the fire
behind her inward-looking sight
in one last blinding light.

Although my heart says she's above,
a sparkling sun,
a new church gleaming love,
at times still since that night I cry,
ice at my core and winter once more.

A translation of 'L'hiver' by Francis Cabrel

The Collector

He collected fluffy toys
and stacked them on his bed:
hedgehogs, dogs and teddy bears
his bestest friends until instead

he collected lego models
that Dad built Christmas Day.
He added spacemen, pirates, knights
who fought, explored and had their way

then he collected football stickers
and swopped them in the yard.
Spanish, Danish, French and Dutch -
the names were really hard.

Collections fill the attic but
the collector's long since gone
collecting beermats, housemates, decades
till The Great Collector comes along.

Orpheus

Don't look back.
His marriage had a second chance
beyond its grave:
the future bright and
governed by the simplest rule.
Don't look back.
He thought of when they first met,
her hair a fiery halo
face ablaze and murmuring his name,
his and only his.
He looked back,
saw her hair turn ashen
heard her mouth some other name
sent her back to Hades.

Putting Family First

When Grandad, Dad and me
tee off
we aim for the same horizon,
swing with the same sweet zing
and follow through.
Perhaps one day my son will do so
too.

Nostalgia: Five Huge Changes in My Lifetime

Blog January 2012

One of the big questions for a writer of historical fiction is how far we can get into the mind of someone who lived centuries ago. Researching facts is not enough; you have to make that imaginative leap into a different way of thought. I am now well into Chapter 3 of writing the follow-up to 'Song at Dawn' and I feel like I'm dancing across twenty tightropes, skipping from one thread to another and testing that they will hold while I turn somersaults and land on my feet. One of those tests is 'Would someone living in that time have behaved in this way?' which adds complications to the usual test question, 'Would this individual have behaved that way or said that?'.

While I was testing my threads, I thought about how much has changed in my own lifetime, making it difficult if not impossible for my children to understand people of an older generation. If you're over thirty, I'm sure you already have a notion of the huge changes to ways of life that we have experienced and at fifty-six, I can add some years to that.

Here is my arbitrary choice of cultural changes in my lifetime (and my white British female cultural background) followed by a very general 12th century take on them:-

1) Children's loss of freedom. People my age had more freedom as children. We had no parental supervision in the parks, in the streets, roaming the countryside, walking (or cycling or taking buses) wherever we chose. Nowadays my parents would be reported to the child protection services but they were considered normal, caring parents in their time. Between the ages of 8 and 11, I met up with friends at dusk and we ran go-carts, chased each other, played gang and spy games, climbed onto roofs, rode each other's bicycles. We went swimming, either as a group or as individuals. I often walked down to the shore alone and swam in the sea. I even remember the sign that said 'No swimming today - sharks' (we were an army family and living in Hong Kong at the time). I caught tadpoles in jamjars by remote waterfalls; I caught buses with my friend to go stationery shopping in the city or village markets. My parents had absolutely no idea where I was and apparently didn't worry. I ran wild and am so grateful for the barefoot richness of my childhood.

12th century (in the regions that are now France and Britain) - Childhood ended young and a child followed in his/her parent's footsteps,

93

heavily gender stereotyped. If you were training to be an archer, you had to start before 8 years old or you'd never be any good. If you were in the landed classes, betrothal at 11 and marriage at 14 were normal. The age of majority was 15.

2) Sex before marriage or - worse still - living in sin doomed a woman forever in this world and the next. Any children resulting were evil.

This was changing in 1970s' Britain but my generation grew up with our parents believing this to be true. They would have been horrified by couples living together and choosing to have children without marrying but this is normal in modern Britain. To be born out of wedlock was a shame that never lifted from my parents' generation. Their peers were locked up in mental asylums for unmarried pregnancy and it was not only the girls who suffered. I know of one 18 year old boy who committed suicide from shame at getting his girlfriend pregnant. These values still hold in other cultures but not in mainstream white Britain. When people complain about the breakdown of marriage as an institution, and the impact on children, it's worth remembering some of the costs of believing that marriage is all, and that a woman's virginity is social currency. No, I don't want to go back to the days when 'living in sin' meant social ostracism.

Part of the same set of values was the attitude to homosexuality, which was illegal between men and unmentionable regardless of gender. There might be a long way still to go but the very existence of a civil partnership shows a huge shift in attitude.

12th century - varied according to social class but virginity (for women) and (arranged) marriage were paramount amongst the nobility. Homosexuality was always condemned in Christian society but a more open feature of men's lives in the Middle East.

3) Global communication meant writing a letter. Using the telephone cost money so I was allowed to give urgent factual messages that way and nothing else. 'Chatting' on the phone was unthinkable. No computers, no cellphones, no texting. We didn't even have one of the newfangled televisions in our house. Photos were expensive, rare and processed in darkrooms, then placed in one or two albums, covering a lifetime with a hundred images. I still remember the excitement when, at fourteen I was given a trannie - a transistor radio. It was about the size of a bag of sugar and I couldn't believe that something that small could work. I used to play Radio Luxemburg late at night, holding this wonderful invention up to my ear when I was supposed to be sleeping.

12th century - the idea of pigeon post was brought back to Europe after seeing this speedy form of communication widely in use in the Holy Land in the middle of the 12th century.

4) Begging on the streets in Britain was rare and confined to a few big cities. We were proud of our social support and our national health care. British people were offended and embarrassed by the dirty foreign habit of begging, that they encountered when travelling.

It is a complete mystery to me as to why there was no-one sleeping rough in the many small towns and villages of Britain that I lived in or passed through when I was growing up. I don't even remember there being people sleeping in doorways and subways in cities, and I was the sort of child who would have noticed. I just don't believe people are poorer today because I remember how poor people were then. Perhaps they had roofs over their heads but were squatting in shed or barns. Perhaps people lived in intolerable situations with each other and had no ideas of escape or living alone. I would really like someone to tell me why this has changed so much. I get the feeling it has changed in Canada too but I don't know about the USA or other countries.

12th century - begging was commonplace, a way of life for many, and there was no provision for the handicapped, the sick or the mentally ill. Beggars were taken for granted and rich people gave alms to beggars as part as their charitable duty. There was no stigma in being a beggar - it was a role in society, albeit at the bottom of the hierarchy.

5) No central heating and little privacy. When the weather became cold, one room in the house was kept warm by an electric/gas/coal fire (the living room), the kitchen was warm from cooking and the rest of the house was brass-monkeys freezing. Washing and bathing in an unheated bathroom in a Scottish winter was the best deterrent to hygiene I've ever known. The hot water bottle was a lifesaver but your nose still turned blue. You could forget going to your bedroom for adolescent sulks; the choice was between the warm living room watching your parents' choice of TV programme (or listening to their Mantovani vinyl LPs), or under-age drinking in the local pub as often as you could manage to escape. Of course if one of your friends had a more teen-friendly house (i.e. their parents were out) you went there. Families were larger and bedrooms were shared so even when the weather was warm, being inside a house meant living too close to your parents, by their rules and preferences.

Nowadays everyone thinks it's his/her right to live alone, which more and more people do. Living with someone else is a huge decision, rather than what used to be considered the natural process whereby you lived with your parents, then you married (and often still lived with your parents).

Central heating allows all the rooms in a house to be used, changing family relations completely. Children and especially teenagers now have a right to privacy, and usually one bedroom per person. Parents and children can avoid seeing each other, even when living in the same house. You can't freeze your kid into being with you any more. And if you don't have shared mealtimes as a routine, which is true of many modern families, you can't starve them into being with you either. Given the choice these days, people spend more time alone - or online with the people they choose to be with - instead of ones in the same house or street.

12th century - Hearth equalled home, whether a cottage with a smoky peat fire and one room to live in or a castle with a fireplace the size of the cottage and a solar, the newly invented main bedchamber. The castles and palaces we love to imagine living in, thinking how grand we would have felt, were actually complete communities housing hundreds of people. It was usual to sleep several in a bed (if you had a bed) and dozens would have slept in the Great Hall. Privacy for procreation was dependent on whether you had the luxury of a curtain between you and your children (or your neighbours). If you were very rich, you would have lived in such a community with a separate bedchamber to yourself, and apart from your spouse, but with servants coming and going all day. Privacy was not a medieval concept. Wanting to be alone would have been considered downright weird and as for the need to 'find yourself' - about as likely as in 1960s' USSR.

In a way, every novel is a historical novel. The time period can never be 'now' as so much is changing technologically, politically and culturally over the time it takes to write and publish 100,000 words. Even fantasy and sci-fi novels have a period feel, based on our current knowledge and technology. Fantasy novels are usually vaguely medieval, with magic added, and follow past conventions about magic. Sci-fi novels imagine the future from the possibilities currently envisioned. You only have to look at sci-fi novels written fifty years ago to see how rooted in their own time they were. So how far we can get into the mind of someone who lived centuries ago seems to me to depend on the usual skills of a writer.

I'd love to hear from other people as to what you think has changed most in your lifetime. If you're under ten, leave it a bit before posting, then get back to me.

Drawn From Your Eyes

Because we two will never live as one,
because our madness ended in two lonely lives,
whatever was, is over now and done -
a million reasons for a million whys
and you should know that - right or wrong -
all my words in every song
draw from the blue-black of your eyes.

I didn't see your well-worn family ties
too dazzled blind the while,
my bonds forgotten, loosed with lies
and dreams of freedom Venice-style
and you should know that - right or wrong -
all my words in every song
reflect the treasure of your smile.

You will forever wander through
my sweetest dreams;
you will forever catch my breath anew
in dawn's rose streams.
And if, in spite of this, I should forget?
I tell you this, that - right or wrong -
all my words in every song
would fill the air with lingering regret.

A translation of 'L'encre de tes yeux' by Francis Cabrel

Bitto

Seven goats his legacy
and when the morning air strums
his lungs, you see him stride the hills
godlike, as, with flute he comes

so you hoped you would ease those black thoughts,
the darkness of fields, of leaves, of earth
and you threw your bare arms, reckless
round the goatherd, mistaking his worth.

*Translated from 'Pan Moderne' by Emile Nelligan and from 'Bitto'
by Anna de Noailles*

The Big Issue

'Why doesn't he run away?' Alun pointed at the dog lying on a stripy blanket in the shoe-shop doorway. The brown mongrel and its owner looked back at him. Neither seemed too willing to waste energy on answering the question. Behind the man and his dog, Alun could see his own reflection shimmering like a ghost among the pairs of shoes, which were stacked in pyramids like a fairground game. If he had a stone with him and chucked it with a bit of spin at the black lace-ups bottom left, he could probably knock the red sandals smack into the bum of the shopper bending to pick up some trainers. Alun's image put its arm back down by his side and his thoughts returned to the question. If nobody answered him at home, he just kept on asking.

'Why doesn't he run away?' he asked again. The man's legs were stretched out in front of him, open, bent at the knees. His arms rested easily on them and he lifted his right hand now and then to take a slow drag. When he lifted his arm, Alun could see a hole in his trouser leg and the frayed ends of a woolly grey sleeve. Some kind of hat lay on the stripy blanket, with a few coins in it, but the man didn't seem to be making much effort to get attention from the passers-by. The dog was lying down, its head resting on crossed front legs. Its eyes guarded the hat and followed the passing shoppers, returning to Alun without much interest.

A second pair of deep brown eyes focused on Alun and the man spoke. 'He's a good dog.'

'Why don't you sell *The Big Issue*?' was Alun's next question.

'Why don't you?' asked the man, in that same slow drawl as if speaking were just another pointless effort. This answer was not nearly as satisfying as the first one and Alun had just opened his mouth to explain why the man should sell *The Big Issue* whereas Alun obviously had no need to, when the man spoke first.

'I gotta go somewhere. Will you look after the dog?'

Alun imagined sitting on the stripy blanket by the dog while the man went shopping. It would be just the same as waiting for his mother, who was taking so long that the man would probably be back before she came. He hoped none of his friends were in town but it would be worth it to talk to the dog. He could say it was a sponsored something. You could get away with anything if it was sponsored.

'All right.' Before Alun could sit down on the blanket, the man had stood, the dog following his movements with its head cocked, fully alert, and the blanket had been folded up. The man took a length of string out of a pocket, tied it round the dog's neck and gave the other end to Alun. The dog listened to the man, whispering something in the dog's ears, which drooped immediately.

'I'll be here again next Thursday,' he told Alun, and disappeared. The dog stood by Alun, waiting for something to happen and Alun stood by the dog, the string clutched tightly. The usual drift of couples, families and kids passed, chattering, but there was no trace of the man. Just as Alun thought his heart would burst from panicked beating, he saw a familiar face - not the man but his mother. This was as bad as it could be.

******

The argument was still going on in the kitchen and Alun could hear his mother's voice, shrill and angry, 'You just encourage him,' and then the lower, more dangerous tones of his father, 'He's only 11, Anne. If you want, we'll take the mutt straight to the vet and finish it off. It's half-starved anyway and there's no pain... just one injection and that's it'.

There was a silence as deep as a dog's brown eyes. Alun sat on the cold patio stone because he thought the dog would feel more at home with someone sitting beside him. The dog gave no sign of feeling anything. It lay beside him in the same pose it had kept on the blanket. If Alun had been braver he would have sneaked a blanket out of the airing cupboard, but one memory of his mother's face when he had tried to explain to her what had happened and he knew the dog would have to lie on the cold stone, at least for now. The silence lasted longer than he could hold his breath, which was a bad sign and very unlucky. He had told himself that if someone spoke before he breathed again then everything would be all right. The next words were spoken too quietly for him to hear but it was his mother's voice. Alun smoothed the dog's short fur, noticing how silky the forehead and ears were compared with the thickness of its back. He wondered how the dog's weatherproofing worked and considered how it would be to have a friend like this, who just sat beside you and thought doggy thoughts.

It was his mother who came out into the garden. Alun was reminded of those films where you saw two characters locked in mortal combat, then you couldn't see them anymore and it was only when the victor emerged that you knew who had won. Except that with his parents there wasn't a goody and a baddy, and it depended what you wanted as to who you wanted to win. And it was always his mother who told him the verdict, whoever had won, so that meant nothing.

'I'm disappointed in you Alun.' This was nothing new. 'You're old enough to have a sense of responsibility. I can't believe you talked to a stranger at all, never mind bringing home a stray.'

'He's not a stray.' A glare from his mother shut him up.

'And we've said no to a dog often enough. But,' she sighed deeply, 'your Dad thinks it's a chance for you to show whether you can look after a pet. We'll try to take him back next week but if you ask me, this con-man just wanted rid of the poor thing, and you'll have had enough so we'll take it to the dog's home then and they'll do what's best.'

******

It was only three days since the dog had moved in but Alun could not imagine life without it. He didn't have to look down to know that the dog was at his side, following his every move, listening to his every word. The string had been abandoned straight away when it became clear that the dog was not going to run away. Quite the opposite: the dog wouldn't run on its own at all. It sat, lay, walked beside Alun, slept where it was told to, and it would even run - beside Alun, if he ran. It was not something he could say to his parents but Alun knew there was something wrong; the dog was just too good.

Day 4 was Sunday, one of those autumn days when the sun gave a last burst of heat and the garden flickered gold. Alun's Dad stopped digging, groaned and stretched to ease his back. He idly threw a stick for the dog, shouting, 'Fetch,' and Alun watched as the dog's eyes followed the stick, while its body stayed rock-still, in its usual working pose.

Dad shook his head and frowned. 'We can't have that on a weekend. Anne?' he called Alun's Mum and went off into the house, emerging minutes later. 'Come on, we're off to the beach. Bring the string, just in case.' Alun, his mother and the dog did as they were told, the back of the car being just another shop doorway as far as the dog was concerned. It didn't wince as Alun's Dad sang along with the car radio, not even when his Mum joined in.

You could always smell the sea, before it appeared as a glint behind a field, hiding with the twists of the lanes and totally invisible from the carpark. Alun cricked his neck round to watch the dog. Perhaps this was its first time. Alun sniffed as if it was his first time; if you covered wet clothes in mud and salt, you still wouldn't come close to the freshness of the wet tang, with a hint of metal and machine from the small railway line which hugged the coast. Had he imagined it? Alun kept watching and sure enough, the dog's nostrils were flickering, twitching with interest, and the fine, straight hairs on the back of its neck were standing up, as if in a breeze which only the dog could feel.

The walk started sensibly, feet and paws moving as in a perfect fire drill, all straight lines and regular pace. Then Dad started zig-zagging and walking backwards, making Mum laugh until she skipped into pigeon steps and wrote his name in huge letters in the sand. Alun veered off his parents' course towards the low breakers, starting to run, his movements shadowed by the dog. They ran into the waves, Alun stopping as the waves lapped the calves of his wellies but the dog continuing to splash in deeper until it was forced to swim. 'You're out of your depth,' Alun told it. The dog carried on swimming. "Dad!" Alun yelled, suddenly afraid, and his father, holding a stick, was suddenly at his side.

'Fetch!' The stick was thrown just in front of the dog's nose and retrieved without hesitation. The dog doubling its clumsy paddles to turn around and bring the stick back. When it reached the shallows, it dropped the stick in front of Alun, wagged its tail and gave a sharp bark. He was slow to understand and the dog nudged the stick with its nose, wagged its tail and barked again.

'Go on, throw it,' his Dad told Alun, and the games began in earnest. In its excitement, the dog turned somersaults in the incoming waves. Even when the dog rushed out of the sea to shower Alun's mother with seawater as it shook itself right beside her, even then there was just shrieking and laughter, as his father encouraged the dog to chase his mother. It had been a long time since Alun had seen his parents playing.

'We'll call him Sandy,' said his mother on the way home and Alun started to hope that they might keep the dog.

But the man was there the next Thursday, just as he had said.

'Where did you go?' asked Alun, despite his mother nudging him. The man just shrugged. 'Were you ill? Are you better now?'

The man looked at him steadily, ignoring his mother, who hovered anxiously beside Alun, not sure of the social rules. 'I wanted the dog to have a holiday. He's too young to understand this life.'

'You've got to give Sandy back, Alun.' His mother was impatient to get it over with but no longer because it was what she wanted.

Alun smoothed the dog's head and sent it back to the blanket with unspoken love. Man and dog greeted each other with a touch, a lick, a tail wag and a smile. 'If you sell *The Big Issue*, my Mum would buy one, wouldn't you Mum?'

'Maybe,' she said.

'So you will sell it then,' Alun persevered.

'Maybe,' said the man, and he turned his attention to the dog, dismissing Alun and his mother even before they turned to go.

*The Big Issue is a newspaper sold by homeless people on the streets of the UK as part of the process to help re-integration into society.

Fruition

In her weary-housewife fifties she had bought
a new expensive fruit from York's best store.
She considered its tough skin then
scored it into four (once for each child)
peeled it back and halved the pear revealed there,
kept the mush-flecked stone to polish later.

The green-gold slices disappointed and
only when the back door opened,
when she paused and met my teenage sister's eyes
and raised that one… last… slice…
the missing flavour gilt her lips.

'Cup of tea?' she asked and no-one named
the strange fruit husked between them.

In riper years, she cherished wooden fruit,
smoothing beech bananas, pearwood apples,
time alone no longer treasured.

Now we know that avocado
was what our mother sampled - and didn't want to share.
Wives and mothers too these days,
we share instead her taste for secret fruit
we know we can't afford.

Someone Else's Kitchen

Here I am again in Someone Else's kitchen.
They leave their breakfast dishes every time
not even soaked. As if I didn't have enough
to do with all that vacuuming.
Cat fluff everywhere! And cats!
They don't mind their pets oh no
as long as Someone Else
does all the cleaning.
Pair of overgrown kids,
that's what they are
and me a paid mother
too skint to say no to
the only job I'm trained for.
More cleaners wanted
than will do the job and me,
I'm not surprised.

Sometimes
I wish I was the Someone Else
who owns the kitchen and
not the Someone Else who cleans it.

Black Hole Blues

A black hole, mass about 100,000 times the sun, is at the centre of our own galaxy.
Stephen Hawking

In London, Jan and Peter's trade was down;
the City sucked its share of stocks and spat
them over Asia, hit the Nikkei fan
en route to Wall Street; poor Japan. Poor Jan
and Peter vacuuming percentage debts

while Sienkin farmed his sheep in Aberconwy
prevented lambing deaths from watery mouth
with bottles of colostrum to compensate
for nature's casual way with profits (30p per lamb
at market price). Why swim against the tide?

Amanda, in her bedroom, felt the black hole's pull
and drew a circle on her belly, her golden ring-pull
shouting that nobody had mothered her; each body part
a fashion statement piercing all the pain of being
fashioned from another's flesh and blood and bone.

And Fran, who lived at Number 10 with all the railings?

Anything could become a black hole if it's squeezed enough.
The less dense the object, the harder it has to be squeezed.

He used to squeeze her, say, 'You're lovely Fran,'
and promise more - in passing - with his sure hands.
He dropped her on her birthday, wishing her
elsewhere. Remembered fingerprints bruised purple
shame from every pore of naked skin.
His absence crushed her; shoulders drooped.
She could not lift her head up, could not.
'You're my squeeze-box, Fran,' he used to say
and she felt light like dancing. They said
she couldn't take the pressure. Yes, that was it.

*After gravitational collapse, a black hole must settle down
into a state in which it could be rotating but not pulsating.*

At ten to HIM her pulse would race; she paced
her breathing by the hall clock but the hands
would dance and side-step up the ante where
she perfumed pulse points, giddy, dizzy,
twirling to his arms; in bed she paced
her breathing to his sleeping rhythm, slowed
her own until her ribs ached amplifying
all the more the joyful throbbing in her cage.

The bottom dropped out of her world and, no-one
left to turn to, she turned regardless
walking streets she didn't know not knowing
why she'd come there, where to turn
and turn again.

*A black hole is a set of events from which it is not possible
to escape to a large distance.*

Fran went by train to London;
she flew by plane to Rome
she changed her job and cut her hair
she partied in her underwear
she laughed as if she didn't care
but all she ran from always won
and monsters chased her home.

She dreamed she was not alone

and Sienkin's sheep were farming stock
which Peter bought and Jan sold
which bankrupt Mandy's Asian Mum
to buy an empty belly's gold.

Can-do

Can't-do could but didn't.
Can-do tried and tried
and ... failed.

'Help me, Can't-do?' Can-do asked.
'Can't,' came the reply.

'Watcha scared of, Can't-do?
What's the worst can be?'

'Failing, feeling stupid,
people mocking me...'

'But you fell and tumbled over
and still you learnt to walk;
you goooed and gaaaaed and babbled
and still you learnt to talk.
We need to get things wrong a lot
to ever get things right,
so help me, Can't-do,
I have tried and tried and
I can't do this alone.
If Can-do can't then maybe
Can't-do can, d'ya reckon?'

'I reckon,' Can't-do smiled,
'two can do better.'

'Yes!'

'Success!'

Lou 2006-2014

The Dogs Who Walk Beside Us

Blog Jan 2014

This wasn't how the story was meant to go. It has been a tough month and Lou died peacefully in my arms on Monday at the vet's after an auto-immune disease had progressively weakened him. I know some of you have grown fond of P'tit Lou from meeting him in my blog and will miss him. You know the French high speed train, the TGV? Well, Lou was a CGV, a Chien à Grande Vitesse. He lived at 100kph, his tail and his heart beating at top speed as he made up for time lost in the animal shelter.

To further complicate my life, while Lou became worse, our Pyrenean Mountain Dog, Blanche, told me there was something seriously wrong so I rushed her to the vet's, jumped the queue and saw the twisted stomach on the X-ray. From the moment I read about this condition in the dog book I translated, I've dreaded it, but the emergency operation was a success and the patient recovered well.

Patient is not the right word for Blanche and she recovered too well for the vet's liking; she trashed everything in her cage and ripped out her stitches during the night after the operation. He called me the next morning asking me to come in and give her tablets, food and a short walk. So I rushed to the vet's again, armed with cooked chicken. It was hard to leave her there another day, for me as well as for the vet, who would have loved me to take her away, but that's when complications can kick in so she did her time. I was told, with professional pride, that the vet managed to give the next dose of tablets and she ate the chicken I left.

She's home now. It was a miracle that all of us reacted so quickly: Blanche, me, the vet. The operation took place before the pain had begun and the prognosis for a full recovery is excellent. The stomach has been attached to the abdominal lining so there shouldn't be any recurrence. Dilation is possible but a comparatively simple problem. I know many people in the dog world who've lost their dogs to a twisted stomach; it's how Blanche's father died. I'm the only person I know with a survivor. Usually a twisted stomach comes on fast and kills quickly.

So here I am with my 8 year old, being lucky, and crying over Lou. Blanche needs to be watched as she treats her Elizabethan collar with total disdain. It's up to the collar to adapt to her ways not vice versa, so if it gets smashed to pieces on the porch door (one collar down and two spares to go) that's hardly her fault. But we've reached Day 6 so we should make it now. And I have time to think about the friend we've lost.

If Lou had known there were only 8 months left for him, I am sure that he would have chosen to spend those months exactly as he did. But he never looked where he was going; he ran full tilt at life and looked back only to check we were keeping up. Several times I had to warn him and he'd swerve in the last minute to avoid smacking into a door or a post, like a cartoon character. I still have no idea how he put a hole in his face but I was there when the emergency vet picked up a stapler and gunned Lou under the eye. Lou hardly flinched, unmuzzled, but when the vet said, 'That didn't go in straight. Hold him while I do it again,' I thought I'd pass out. The vet did it again. Straight. And Lou took it. Straight.

A friend's favourite Lou story is what she calls 'the curious incident of the hose in the daytime'. Two rubber snake-monsters attacked Lou in the outer garden and I witnessed Superdog defending himself single-pawed, biting their heads off and refusing to let go, despite the torrents of water drenching him. Unfortunately, I found out about a second such attack at the moment a mudbath with paws arrived in our living room and shook itself. John reckons Lou was a reincarnation of Riki-Tiki-Tavi.

Lou was a lesson in living well. He knew how to have fun. He won his Princess from polite beginnings to no-holds-barred play. He found it entertaining to take all the dog blankets off the veranda onto the lawn and he trained us to retrieve them. He thought he'd won if he had Blanche's blanket, even if his head was in her mouth at the time. When he was ill, especially as he became worse, she'd come in from guard duty and lie near him, facing him, so they could look at each other.

When someone dies, our reaction is based so much on the human perception of time. A life is often perceived as 'cut short', a death is 'untimely' and 'unfair', all based on life 'expectancy', which is of course an average. Yet we all expect to reach average, even though we know this is statistically stupid. When we lose our dog, there is a clash between two different time scales that worsens this sense of unfairness. With Lou, eight months as a proportion of my life is so small. 'Unfair' seems even more unfair with a rescue dog who 'deserves' compensation for the bad times. And if, like me, you go through this heartache with several dogs, you find it hard to accept that it is impersonal. The laws of probability mean a penny can come up heads 99 times and the odds of heads for the 100th time are still 50:50.

When we live with animals we must live with different time scales and it is hard to deal with all the deaths that must come our way when dogs walk beside us throughout our averagely long lives. There is not just a clash of scale but of world view. In his powerful and intelligent book 'The Philosopher and the Wolf', Mark Rowlands explores the experience of time for a wolf, as opposed to conventions of time for us humans, and shows what we can learn. I think he is right. My grief remains but I am already losing the sense of unfairness. If 'quality of life' (lack of) is the touchstone for choosing euthanasia, then surely quality of life is equally the touchstone for living. Not some construct we call time. Not some linear notion. Lou was not chasing the future. He was running because it was wonderful to run. And for a while, we ran together. And it was so good.

'It is in our lives and not, fundamentally, in our conscious experiences that we find the memories of those who are gone. Our consciousness is fickle and not worthy of the task of remembering. The most important way of remembering someone is by being the person they made us - at least in part - and living the life they have helped shape. Sometimes they are not worth remembering. In that case, our most important existential task is to expunge them from the narrative of our lives. But when they are worth remembering, then being someone they have helped fashion and living a life they have helped forge are not only how we remember them; they are how we honour them.

I will always remember my wolf brother. '
Mark Rowlands, 'The Philosopher and the Wolf'

Lou playing the matador with his 'little white bull'

International Love Spoon

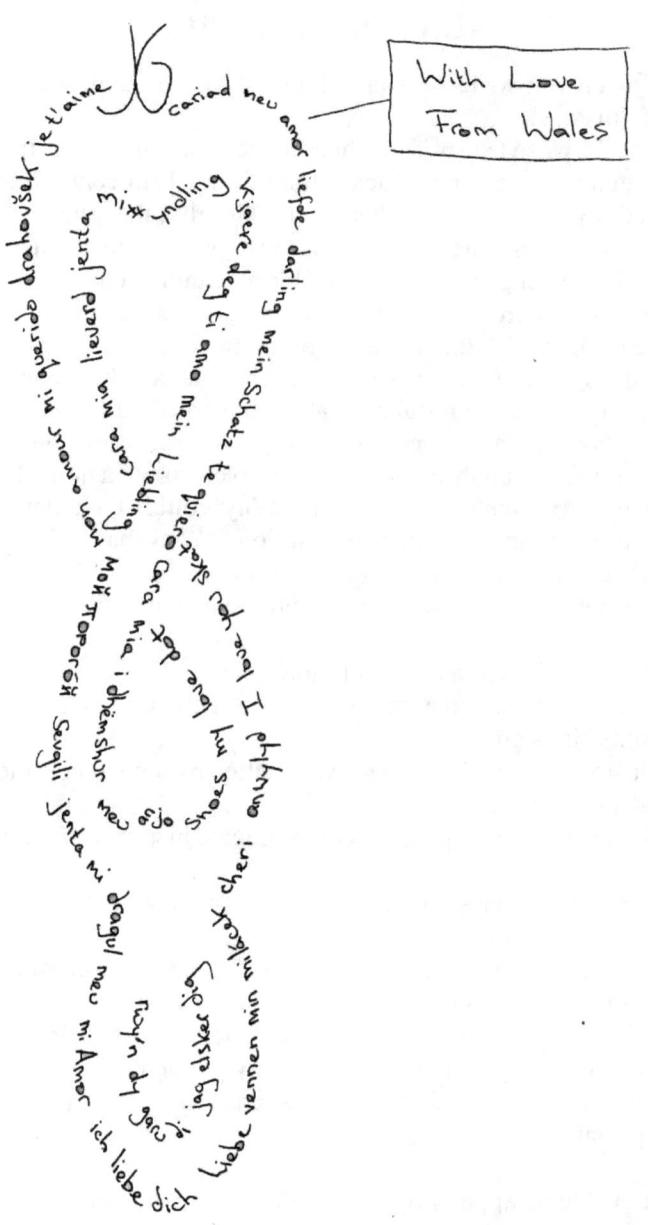

With Love From Wales

Let's Argue About History

Blog Post Jan 2013

W hen you write a historical novel, you can expect to argue about history.

I wasn't surprised when my network of critical friends found some mistakes in the period background of my 12th century novel and it was incredibly useful to have their input. Usually, they were right.

What did surprise me though was how passionate I felt about some aspects of my background research: black armour, chastity belts, riding side-saddle, handkerchiefs, pills, sweets and Damascene swordmaking are just some of the topics that raise my blood pressure.

Sometimes, I really did have evidence that bucked the received opinion. Sometimes I just felt plain stubborn about the practicalities of life. I haven't felt like this since a historian told me that prehistoric men did cave-drawings of prey animals either to plan or to celebrate a hunt. 'How do you know they were men?' I asked him. 'Why couldn't women have been drawing to entertain and teach the children?' And that's if you assume a patriarchal gender-stereotyped society. What if it wasn't?

In a nutshell, these are some of the problems with 'history'

- Evidence is limited and open to interpretation.
- Theories are based on assumptions - and collapse like a house of cards if the assumptions are changed.
- The history passed down to us was written by men, and is mostly about male leaders - HIS story.
- Different places and peoples communicate history differently.

So, in random order - and feel free to comment:-

chastity belts - were they around in 1150 and what were they used for? I found some online suggestions that the Crusades of 1147 onwards, resulting in husbands' long absences, motivated the use of chastity belts. I like the idea that they were perhaps used by women to prevent rape rather than by husbands to lock up their wives' chastity but I don't see why both can't be possible.

handkerchiefs - apparently not around in 1150 but what I want to know is whether this just means that the word hadn't been coined or whether people all wiped their noses on their sleeves? Just because there's no evidence of something doesn't mean it wasn't there and I don't believe that inventive individuals didn't ... invent!... useful items ahead of their official appearance in language or records. If I'd lived in the 12th century, I'd have had a nose-wiping scarf! As well as a pretty no-snot one to give to my true knight.

the Black Knight - OK, no black armour in 1150 (although I bet the Japanese Samurai had some) but everyone who's watched 'Monty Python and the Holy Grail', or of course read the Mabinogion, knows that the black knight is the baddy. So what was black about him? No, I don't believe it was just his black heart showing.

riding side-saddle - didn't happen until much later, when the saddle for riding in this manner was invented. Pictures show women in medieval Europe riding astride. I agree that, women rode astride! However, that doesn't mean they never rode side-saddle. Absence of proof doesn't mean it didn't happen. And have you tried sitting astride a horse, while wearing a long, slightly flared gown? You have to hitch your skirt up to your knickers (which you wouldn't have been wearing in 1150) and, believe me, the pose is really not ladylike. So, unless you were wearing your incredibly wide circular riding-gown, I reckon you'd have gone for sitting side-saddle! I have found one person who agrees with me - hooray!

pills, sweets and Damascene swordmaking - not known in northern Europe in 1150. Agreed. But it is difficult for someone British (me) to take in just how sophisticated al-Andalus (Muslim-occupied Spain) and the Holy Land were in 1150. The Arabs, other Middle Eastern peoples, and the Jews, wherever they lived, had highly developed science, medicine, surgery, engineering, geography. They could definitely make pills and sweets.

Britain had no sugar. This luxury only reached southern France in 1150, reportedly brought back from the crusades by Alienor (Eleanor) of Aquitaine, which no doubt changed sweet and dessert possibilities.

The superb filigree swords of Damascus, combining strength and beauty, cannot be recreated today. Scientists think that one of the ingredients, probably coming from India, was exhausted so that it is no longer possible to recreate the chemistry.

Any Christians trading with other peoples, or crusading against them - especially those who settled in the Holy Land - came into contact with all this knowledge. They brought it back to the south of France in 1149, to barbaric Britain at the end of the 12th century. And the Church stamped out every example of 'heresy' it found, from papermaking to astronomy.

I would like to believe that individuals like my character, Dragonetz, learned from their neighbour Moors and Jews, and that little candles of knowledge were passed on, despite the Church, to blaze into the Christian community's collective mind two hundred years later. We did finally, get books for everyone. And now look what's happening to them.

Theory of Relativity

Like a plug-in model of atomic structure
one to one is simplest; add one -

four possible combinations and
ongoing, simultaneous, exclusive or explosive.

Add one more, etcetera.
There were six of us to cross-connect or add.

When the children left
your unplugged arms ached with absence

like amputated limbs.

To Be a Pilgrim

(Rocamadour, France)

If you seek wisdom
look long at a stone
until you see its many faces
until it moves.

Rock of ages virgin cleft
the black Madonna in her chapel
cleaves to rock
the Church's rock.
The Church is rocking
but the pilgrims kneel still
step by bruising step in penance
past Durandal's tourist shop
where Roland's sword sells key-rings.

Five hundred prayer candles sweat.
There aren't so many marble thanks
although they plate a wall, initialed
or anonymous; thanks for someone
safe from war; for some boat safe ashore,
from Jacques and friends cured 1536
of fever. Hail Mary, Notre Dame du Haut Mont.
There is a place within the prayer format
where you may place a personal insertion.
The customary phrase is Gimme Gimme Gimme
please and I'll be good.

Incense mixed with bitumen drifts
up towards the Stations of the Cross
where tar repairs black-patch the footpath.
Saint Veronique at Number Six
'a pious lady washes Jesu's face'
is long outsainted by her husband's relics.
Buried underneath the rock he loved
and lived on, widowed hermit,
Saint Amatore, Rock- and Mary-lover.
He lay eleven hundred years

across the chapel threshold boning up
to sainthood, alchemised to stone.
Honed femurs and some polished shards
brought Europe to its knees.

It's named in Occitan, the tongue of Oc
its hard yes almost roc. Rocamadour
is best viewed from the air by saints
and eagles.

Man flung me from his leather glove
to hang
between the freedom and the flight
to circle
over cliffs and green-bed valley
to drop
and drink the rabbit's scream.
My rock they name this, little men
as if there were a high place
worth the name, not eagle's.
We, loving rock, made pacts;
wing out as raptors to regard the rapt.

We saw the kings and queens competing
in their pious acts, their public show,
requests for treaties safely made or
(more like common folk) an heir.

We saw those punished into pilgrims,
recanting Cathars fearing for their lives.
Their penitential fetters dragged them down
to plead permission for a sanctioned life
of sorts.

All bring their prayers up to the Goddess
sister to the one we saw in Crete
whose outstretched hands held snakes.
This Mary grips her throne of Wisdom, has
no contact with the son who rises
from her lap, his simian face an adult's.

From the chapel ceiling swings

the legendary bell, still.
Ding dong dell
ring the miracle, tell
the gullible I tolled
the oracular bell.
When someone takes your chains off
do you find you miss the weight?
When someone says, 'Go sin no more,'
which sins d'you contemplate?
When you're told that you're forgiven
does it seem to you that even if
you are
you'd rather not live by the rules we've
had by chance which in their stance
are quite unbearably bizarre.

The tourist mother rocks her baby
an instant's grace before the cry.
Up above the castle ramparts
the two-thirty eagles soar
to catch the sun, then dive.
Rock the foundation
dissolve crumble cave.

Park Statue

Cast iron,
like Marilyn Monroe
skirt flaring high
face mis-shapen in a greying wind
bare-foot in the cold
a homeless beauty cast
in foundry flames
to star in the park
between 'NO LITTER!'
and 'KEEP OFF THE GRASS'
while the park-keeper stabs
the litter, walks his heron stalk,
checks for bad boys in the toilets.

And if one night she smooths her hair
and twirls her skirt and dances barefoot
will the locked gates tell the stars?

Wedding Cake

The icing tasted sweet once;
years hardened sugar crust
to frosting.

Know That I

'I love you' has so many shades:
not just love, not only that,
dragging time into the line
you sign on, saying those three words.

You speak of love in its own tongue:
for me these words lose any point
if you need them said as hostages,
a seal on parchment.

So you should know that
I -
Know that
I -

There is 'till death' in 'I love you'.
There is 'I see no-one but you';
dead to the world, to its poetry,
reading only of yourself.

A dishonest stratagem,
no affirmation in these words:
the question rather in 'I love you'-
'do you love me back, do...?'

So you should know that
I -
Know that
I -

A translation of 'Sache que je' by Jean-Jacques Goldman

Not What You Think

It's the easy questions that you can't answer, like 'Where are you from?' What do you say? You've moved so often you've lost count and you only stayed six months where you were born. If you're feeling tactful (rare) you say you've moved a lot but you were born in … If you're feeling 'difficult' (your mother's word) you tell them, 'Nowhere' or shrug and say, 'I don't know.' You'll find it matters, to them.

'How many children do you have?' Three steps, one adopted, one grown from a seed - part-shares in five. You know it's not the answer that they want but still it's one to warm the heart that once fielded, 'Do you have any children?' You have a friend who always says, 'Four but one's dead.' Your heart has seven children but you know not to say so. Times change; you've come from gloves at Sunday school and nice-girls-don't, to embryos on hold and suicide by cop. A new one, that. You think of a policeman as a loaded, lethal weapon and you pull the trigger - something like 'Hey Officer Dibble, your mother was a teacher', or some such intolerable jibe. Then 'Bang!' you're dead, such is the quality of arms training for American police. Even with gun-toting detectives, I don't think it would be as reliable in Britain, particularly if you're white.

So I'm middle-aged; middle-ennial in the new millenium; mid-enemal. And just when I thought I'd put the 'f' in 'jaded' (haven't you been f''in jaded?) along came Jones. This being Wales meant that the Jones bit was not such a surprise. Everything else about him was.

At three minutes past one, on a July Tuesday when the rain was just holding off, I was mowing the big lawn and spending my lottery millions. I had just started an imaginary argument with my husband over whether we should set up a trust fund to pass money on to the ten relatives also-known-as close, or give lump sums to them and never mind the tax (my ideas), or (his idea) forget the buggers now and they'd get more when we died, soon, of luxury-induced apoplexy, when I had a vision. More of an aud-ion really because it was only a voice-over. I didn't even look for a neighbour hiding behind a hedge or a helicopter within speaking distance, which I just might have missed in my absorption, because it was really not that sort of voice. It was as if only one speaker of a Walkman was working and the volume jammed on just one little black line too loud. The voice said, 'Should we keep men as pets any more?'

Like most of us, I'd always tried to think of men as equals; until I heard that voice I *thought* I thought of men as equals. Clever technique, mind you; the 'any more' distracts you from questioning the initial premise that we do keep men as pets, while spotting the distraction and the premise makes you take the question seriously, and before you know where you are, you've been seriously discussing the question - with yourself - for long enough to allow the question to exist. There are people who can just say, 'Eh?' but I am not one of them. I left the lawn on half and went in for a cup of tea.

'Michael,' I said.

'Yes?' He was watching Arsenal versus InterMilan, a team which is not as good as A.C.Milan. It is sometimes useful to know such things.

'Do you sometimes feel as if men nowadays are kind of like pets? I mean boys aren't doing as well in school and there will be more women than men in work in the 21st century and there are more men in prison and rapists and stuff and I know they - the scientists - say it's got nothing to do with testosterone and you do wonder, don't you?' Pause. 'Well?'

'What was the question again?'

'Are you a pet?'

'I should say so. Have you finished the lawn?'

'Not yet.'

'Do you want a hand?' Said without discernible body movement although if taken up on the offer, he would certainly have fulfilled it, and cheerfully, to be fair - like a dog going walkies on a rainy day.

'No thanks, I can manage.'

During the 13th vertical stripe (my preferred route created two short 'horizontal' stripes at each end for turning the mower and 17 long 'vertical' stripes) the voice said, 'You're not too old for abandoned sex.'

That was when I started talking back.

I *thought* that I probably should have abandoned sex many years ago but what I *said* was 'Bugger off.'

As always, any reply only encouraged a stranger. This one became even stranger and very familiar. 'Call me Jones'

'Bugger off, Jones.'

And then Jones started again. 'Why are you so scared of the future?'

I bit back the 'B' in 'Bugger' and settled on petulance. 'Don't know what you mean.'

'So what's the worst you can imagine?'

That was easy. I gave him polluted seas radiating sickness to swimmers and seafood; kids' lungs corroded by steroid inhalers to help them gasp in the filthy air; the privileged classes cocooned in their mechanised homes, arranging AIDS-free partnerships over the INTERNET, increasingly sterile or too self-contained to breed; the majority of the human race shooting up in dingy doorways or dusty savannahs, reducing the life-style and -span of dogs to their own; climatic swings to drown and blast and melt what was left of the earth before the sun exploded. I ran out of breath, not words.

'You have no imagination. That's just how it is now. What is the best you can imagine?'

'No ironing.'

Jones gave one of those ostentatiously patient sighs which shows that someone finds you difficult. 'Try harder.'

'Good health for all.'

'Not enough.' Then the world-swirling began. What I hate about an out-of-body experience is the psychedelic sickness of transition to wherever. Or in this case, whenever.

Before you could say, 'Not now Jones, I've got a headache,' I was angelically poised over a sort of swimming pool. It was a state-of-the art theme pool but instead of the usual multi-coloured plastic erections signifying, 'Fun, fun, fun', there were grey rocks etched with pale pink strata, pebble-smooth around small pools and craggy higher up, further from the water. The water itself was cobalt instead of varnish-with-a-hint-of-blue. Its depths were unfathomable, with no glimpses of hyphenated lane-lines. Ripples broke gently on the rocks, presumably from a wave machine. If it were not for the cloudy blue ceiling and neutral walls on three sides, the illusion of a rocky beach at high tide would have been totally successful. I could even smell salt freshness and it struck me that I had given up swimming in the sea, too conscious of sewage pollution and the risks of gastroenteritis or something worse. They, future-people, seemed to have solved that problem with a very tasteful simulation. As I had predicted, the rich would sense life from behind thick glass walls, while out there Planet Earth and the rest of humanity died.

A movement by the fourth wall, which was furthest away from me, drew my attention. The whole wall was a trompe-l'oeil depiction of rocks opening out to sea, with small boats visible on the imaginary horizon. The painted sky even had cotton-wool clouds drifting across - laser lighting or some such trickery. It was difficult to distinguish what was moving at the far end of the pool, which must have been fifty yards away, but something was moving swiftly towards me through the water.

I turned at a noise behind me to see a door open and a young woman in skin-tight not-skin, pick her way carefully across the rocks towards the pool. In the manner of those to whom 0.001 of a second makes the difference between a gold and a silver medal, she was entirely shaven. I assumed that this was for streamlined swimming rather than an evolution of species, but what amazed me was seeing her all-over smoothness - and I mean *all* over - unhindered by whatever passed for a swimsuit these days. Jones gave one of those gulps which bore no relationship whatsoever to the sigh I'd aroused earlier. Old lecher.

'Your great grand-daughter,' remarked Jones.

Perhaps there was a likeness; she was, after all, a very attractive girl. She wriggled into the water to join the moving body that she could never match in speed, turns or water wisdom. The eternal smile of a dolphin breached and leapt over the girl, who arched and dived in her turn, relaxed in a familiar pattern of choreographed moves. So they still imprisoned the world's most intelligent creatures for demeaning show, and my descendant was a pretty, aquatic zoo-keeper turning tricks for any audience.

My contempt was not at all influenced by the fact that I'd always wanted to swim with dolphins and never had. I'd read all the stories; you know, the Greek boy who swam with his dolphin every dawn to greet the day and whose girlfriend was so torn with jealousy she made him choose - legend said you'd see him out in the bay every dawn, dancing with dolphins, but he was never seen on land again; the survival tales of swimmers piloted and pulled to safety through shark-infested waters; the darker revelations about Cold War dolphin spies which were trained to kamikaze head-butt underwater saboteurs, fatally detonating the spikes attached to the dolphins' heads. Then there's the media performance. Thousands of pounds are raised to help autistic children swim with dolphins and speak their first word ever in the best moment of their lives, so we can read about it in our daily papers, pleasantly moist-eyed, while the children's parents spend the rest of their lives begging for enough money to repeat the moment. Merely miserable buggers like me have no chance, not unless we jump off our chosen cliff at the precise moment a dolphin is passing.

Perhaps, in this future-world, they'd finally tapped the medicinal potential of dolphin contact. You only have to think briefly about the aesthetic abuse of water known as synchronised swimming to realise *why* we want to see dolphins, but it's more than that. I think it's the miracle of them still trying to make contact with us, the patient triumph of ancient optimism over centuries of cruel experience. What you want and what you should do have never been best friends; I wanted to be that girl playing with her friend in the water but I thought it entirely wrong to treat an intelligent being as a performing … a performing … animal.

Squeaks familiar to me from nature documentaries were echoing round the pool chamber and there was that feeling of frustration when you know someone's speaking, let's say in Russian, and you can even recognise what the language is, but you don't know what she's saying. It's always been like that when I've heard my dogs whine and bark, but it's even more the case with nature's most complex languages like whalesong.

You feel you should be recording it onto staves, then turning the pattern into a regular poetical form and that the combination of Music, Maths and Poetry would suddenly make, not just sense, but SENSE. I just wished I knew what the dolphin was saying.

'She does,' said Jones. 'Listen.'

I've never done drugs and regular, moderate alcohol intake should not result in hearing a conversation between a human and a dolphin. Note that by now all other aspects of the Jones affair seemed perfectly normal, such is our capacity to accept whatever is least weird.

When I listened more carefully, I could hear two voices making the characteristic squeals and chirrups as girl and dolphin played chase and tickle-your-tail. As if there were a tuning adjustment in my overstretched brain, I could make out the gist of a dialogue which seemed to work in emotional resonances rather than words. It's difficult to explain but just think how different 'Je t'aime' feels from 'I love you'; now try and imagine the same statement translated into Bushman clicks, with all the cultural baggage that is part of a language; now try to think dolphin.

I'd expected the same sort of conversation I'd had with my dogs; you know, 'Who's a good girl then.' (Tail wags, excited noises). And so on. Instead I listened to a discussion of the health of the world's oceans, as reported to their messenger by the dolphins on patrol. Apparently, there was concern over a shift in the Gulf Stream and a request for an adjustment to weather control by the humans; a glut of cod in the Atlantic showed the success of the past two years' fishing ban and it was time to trawl again; Antarctic whales reported effective re-icification and there was news of good seal-floes in the Arctic - all in all, a tribute to the Partnership.

The girl warned - him? her? of a malfunctioning treatment plant and suggested a re-route for travelling orca. Recovery of radiation waste was progressing off Bikini Atoll for standard disposal into M2467. ??? I asked Jones.

'I'll try and put it simply for you. They've discovered that at a particular stage some stars sort of eat radiation waste and they are able to project the waste using new rocket technology, into the star's gravitational field. There's been a universal clean-up, including the oceans, landfill sites and all the garbage that your generation left floating in near space. Oh yes, and they've also developed nuclear power so that a generator the size of a laptop powers all the electricity needs of a country - for every country. With safe waste disposal, it's a doddle - after all, atoms are *the* renewable resource.'

Severe brain overload. 'Nope, not possible. This does not compute.'

'Do you remember all those loony dreams you and your friends had in the seventies? How you were laughed at for talking about recycling paper and glass? Or the idea of lead-free petrol? The rate of the acceleration of change is accelerating faster.' That was one step too far for me; statistical analysis of second differentials I can cope with, but of third?

He continued, 'You can't begin to imagine the science that has made this world cleaner, healthier and a natural haven. Even in your day you could see that there were more cars on the road than was practical and you already had the solution - the internet and virtual communication. It was just a question of changing working habits, indeed changing work. This is her work.'

As I watched, more black shapes appeared, not by the back wall as I'd first thought, but through it. Limited by expectation, I had not seen that there was no back wall. I had found it easier to see an illusion than to observe that the swimming pool was completely open to the sea, allowing dolphins to come and go. No, not just open to the sea - the swimming pool was sea. Far from being an incredible work of artifice, the room was a basic three-sided shelter round a small cove, creating a Dolphin-Human Conference Centre. Not a miracle of technology then, although the structure was an engineering feat in size, but a sea-change, one dolphin leap for mankind.

'She's special you know. Even now, not many have her gift for languages, nor her political nous.'

The cool blue light glinted on a jewel at the girl's throat and I instinctively reached for its twin around my own neck, my grandmother's sapphire.

'She shouldn't wear that in the water; it'll come loose from its setting.'

'You sometimes pass on more than you know to the next generation,' Jones told me.

You either had to stay there forever or have one peek only and Jones gave me no choice. Dolphins and girl swirled into world change and we were off again.

I sat down with a bump on the raised flowerbed and contemplated a very abandoned lawnmower. There's some native tribe who always draw people walking backwards into the future, able to see only what's past, which seems a much better image than 'looking to the future'. If I hadn't been there and seen just a tiny amount of its impossibility, I'd still be predicting with the worst of them, thinking that what *is* creates what could be.

'You have nice hair,' said Jones with all the warm Welshness that has purred sexuality into Shakespearian lines that nobody understands and everyone wants to hear again - said in just that way.

'Who told you I was too old?' I leant back, undoing the buttons on a thin blouse, unzipping my shorts and posing provocatively. I'd have been all right as a stripper if the audience had been disembodied warm voices - I enjoy the wriggling and self-display, in a narcissistic sort of way, but I don't like people watching. Give me a mirror and a dance record, on a good day. This was a particularly good day.

'Have you finished mowing the lawn?' asked Michael, regarding my unbuttoned state with definite interest. Presumably it was half-time so he had come outside to check on the lawn and me, not necessarily in that order. He was the sort of man who was always helpful with any little jobs I wanted done and for the second time in my life - or how would we be together? - not only was he the right man but he was in exactly the right place at the right time. Not unobservant at such times, he took with enthusiasm the opportunity presented.

Lying amid crushed bergenias, we realised that it had started to rain. No chance of finishing the lawn.

'Thank you,' I murmured into Michael's ear and kissed him.

'My pleasure,' said Jones.

The Gynaecologist's Wife

The problem's not as you would think
his lust for clients but

his clinical detachment
naked in my bed.

And then I bought the screen,
I called him 'Doctor',

dropped my knickers out of sight
and offered him my full blown rose.

I asked my love - as women always have -
Am I all right? Am I as good as them? Am I?

And he said, yes, oh yes
and did without the gloves.

Leaving the Treasures of Earth

What could I send you
when they said how very ill you were
but earth's most precious fruit
fresh dug from Alba's soil, my motherland.
Food of gods, of kings, of pigs, our common love;
for you too were invited to the mushroom feast
despite your English countryside
where fungi flaunt their witching past, grow huge,
contemptuous of their cousins' continental fate,
more often kicked than picked.

I have gathered ceps for England
but my solitary basket could not fill
the plates of those who trust in shiny cafés
and fear the darkness under trees.
They came to me, the Polish refugees
with baskets and with peasant sureness
knowing Caesar's mushroom from the death cap.
The English do not know the quiet hunt,
the weekend train from Moscow to the woods
and back at night to feed the city.

But you were always more than English and
I sent you truffles daily for your last two months.
You sniffed my male pig hormones, knew me friend
and sharer in the treasures of the earth.
Like oak and truffle, our mycorrhizal link
has roots in fields and food. Mycelia live long,
the spores will spread and though we leave earth's riches
we leave them to our children
and decay is just a whiff of truffle.

(for Antonio Carluccio, the television chef and mushroom expert,
after I heard him telling this story of his friendship with Jane
Grigson, another great food writer, author of 'The Mushroom Feast')

Mother Tongue

The piper plays
'I will return no more'
(a Scottish lament requested by Rob Roy
to die to). I'm not Scottish
though my parents were,
though auld words keen like bagpipes
in their rolling hills and r's.
I cast no clout till May be oot;
I hang my washing only in a druith.
My sick child's peely-wally
wi' a glakit look. When well,
he plowters in the mud
as I did once, when wee.
The Scottish flag's a bonny colour;
if Ah wear tartan, Ah'm entititled.
Ach there's a lot of blether talked
on purple-headed mountains.
D'ye ken the song God wrote?
His own country we are.
Ah mind he played his own accordion then
afore the Songs of Praise
and spoke the Gaelic - whit else?
My childhood other country,
I will return no more.

*Dialect words
cast no clout till May be oot - leave off no layer of clothing till the
May (hawthorn) blossoms/until the end of May (the month) - proverb
druith - drying wind
peely wally - sickly
glakit - glazed (expression)
plowters - plays in mud or water
blether - chatter

*Songs of Praise - a popular UK television programme
of hymn-singing

Cross Words

A Bad Night with The Times Cryptic

Five letters.
Seething initially and
you're mad then changed
say non-you, are
filled with regret.

Answer on page 155.

A Taste of Honey

Blog May 2014

First you buy a plot of land in Provence, complete with an old beehive. Then you go on a beekeeping course, where you meet people whose idea of fun is turning up at an emergency swarm alert. Like fishermen and hunters, they tell you horror stories to check whether your testosterone level is high enough to pass the test. So I've heard about the man who suddenly became allergic after twenty years. Died. And the man who tried to speak after swallowing a bee - the swelling closed his respiratory channels. Died. And don't ever ever go in with the bees during a storm - they are 'méchants', 'wicked'. Despite all this, I have now enjoyed 4 days of hands-on beekeeping lessons. Gloved hands-on, as far as I'm concerned.

The same experts who swop these stories handle bees without gloves and leave their face masks down, while we debutantes naively - and cheerfully - avoid getting stung. My beemaster - we'll call him OBee (because I feel like I'm being taught how to use the force) told me, 'Nobody ever forgets the first time he (or she) goes in with the bees...'

My first time was on a windy day, when an old hand said she wasn't touching the bees in that weather. It wasn't so much that my testosterone levels were up as that I didn't want another fortnight 'looking forward' to it. I had no idea how I would react mentally, although physically I'm not allergic (in theory - there are always the horror stories...). We were doing the spring check so I took my turn to lift up each frame in turn, check for the brood cells, honey and pollen. Later I would learn to distinguish between the cells: workers, drone and queen (sign of swarm preparation); young and old.

Advice I wish I'd been given before going in with the bees? Wipe your nose - it will run, the minute you're trapped in a bee jacket and mask. Tie your hair back. Your hair gets in your eyes, your glasses slip down your nose and if you prod at your face through the mesh you're likely to draw blood or squash a bee against your skin. The funniest thing I've seen is someone answering a mobile phone through a bee outfit.

The bees were in a filthy mood from the wind and when I was holding a frame, one stung me through my glove - welcome to beekeeping. I was too interested to be scared and if I focused on the activities round me rather than individual bees flying by my face, I could ignore the angry dive-bombing and tapping at my mask. Until my instinct told me that a bee was inside my mask, not outside . 'Paranoia,' I thought. 'Fact,' my more sensible perception told me. 'Yikes,' I thought, as I focused on said bee hitching a ride on the inside of my face mask. I walked a long long way from the angry hives and luckily my pet bee was calmer than I felt (rather than showed). She flew off when I took off the jacket and released her. Then I did a real 'Yikes' dance. And another one when I was given the advice on not opening your mouth when a bee can go into it. So that's what could have happened, I tried not to think.

Another piece of advice that came too late for one of my classmates was to check very carefully for unwanted company when you remove your protective clothing. It's a bit like climbers falling off a mountain on the way down; beekeepers get stung when they've finished working. Your guard is down, you're a long way from the hives and you don't notice the one bee sitting on your shoulder/head/glove. They're attracted by the lovely smells you've acquired while raiding their hive and they travel with you a long way. When OBee turned up at my house in his battered 2CV, I noted the one obligatory bee in the back of his car - like taking your dog out with you.

I came off lightly from that first session compared with the lively nine year old who'd insisted on accompanying his father, didn't sit far enough away from the action and was stung several times on his bare head. Health and safety is different in Provence. Sheltering in a car after that, the little boy was sharp-eyed at spotting bees still clinging to clothes, but as he screamed 'Kill it!' every time he saw one, I feel that the lesson was counterproductive for his future as a conservationist.

Since then, I've made progress with my own bees and will give you all the detail on that, next blog post. I also bought the full spacesuit outfit, after my moment with interior bee. My face could be improved, but that is not how.

I love saying MY bees. Readers of *How Blue is my Valley* will remember the old beehive on the hillside, here in Provence. Since I wrote about it, we scraped together enough cash to buy the orchard, complete with truffle oaks and bees, but lacking truffles (or we could never have afforded it).

Crazy Jane Heeds the Words
of the Poet and the Playwright

Her bats haunt the bench where they sit
so she joins the two writers, stilling
the black zooms and swoops of her mind.

'Bats … have we a bat poem?'
He flicks the book through, searching.
The poet flings quotations in the air;
the playwright shoots them down with ease
while Crazy Jane listens to their talk.

The morning sun had not been hers it seemed
but someone Cary's 'orange among fish'.
Yet she had known the sun.
Their chat on writing carries on,
'Edit out hellos, how are yous, weather comments,
they're only ways of writing yourself in …'

Their search for words reflected hers for living
but less real. Without writing herself in
she had known a man in sunlight.
Crazy Jane heeded their words, worried
that she too would become literary
not just bats.

Thannenkirch (Alsace)

Meet me at the crossroads of
the black cherry tree in the pines.
Walk by the way-marked path
that winds from blossom to dark firs.

Look back before the bend;
the church tower points Germanic
to the village roofs of slate
still shining from late snow.
Two storks migrating northwards
circle, searching out a twiggy crown.
Diminished log-piles, stacked
methodically by homesteads
feed the fires I'll hold you by.
Of mountain water turned to wine
in long-stemmed flutes, green-rimmed,
hand-etched with graven flowers,
we'll sip the future dry.

Harvest of '92

Alsace wines taste miraculous of water.
The drops we kissed below your hat
matured October in the nailbiting wait
on weather by our viticulteur host.
No walking in the rain for him, instead
the vintner's magic; recognise the moment
that grape must quit vine, turn elixir
for the likes of you and me to taste
another vintage raindrop year.

John

in Aristotle's nine categories by which an object can be regarded

Quantity: Man, one

Quality: Well-tempered, sterling, proved and weighed, albeit in kilograms

Relation: My Gamekeeper, Groundsman, Gardener, Sous-chef, Chief Crossword-Solver, Deputy Dog-Walker, Fan, Critic, Bodyguard, Husband, Partner, Best Friend Forever

Position: Contractual

Place: On his terroir among the Provençal vines below the beehive terrace

Time: Three of the clock on a Thursday afternoon

State: Perpetual Motion

Action: Beheading les herbes with a right-handed strimmer that stutters and chokes

Affection: Always, my love. Affecting everything we do.

Review my book or else . . .

If you liked my book, please help other readers find it by writing a review. Thank you.

Contact Jean Gill

I love to hear from readers. Email me at jean.gill@wanadoo.fr

Blog: news, views, tips and trivia at www.jeangill.blogspot.com where you can meet Sherlock, the abandoned hunting-dog we adopted.

Check out my website www.jeangill.com
My photos are for sale at www.istockphoto.com/jeangill
Twitter @writerjeangill
Facebook www.facebook.com/writerjeangill

Recommendations, if you would like to read another book by Jean Gill:

If you want to read more about my life in France, try *How Blue is my Valley*. Humorous travel/autobiography about my first year living in Provence and how it compared with Wales. Amazon uk No1 bestseller in 2013.

'Laugh out loud in many places... such a vivid picture of fields of lavender, sunflowers and olive trees that you could almost be there with her.' **Living France Magazine**

The true scents of Provence?
Lavender, thyme and septic tank.
How can you resist a village called Dieulefit, `God created it', the village 'where everyone belongs'. Discover the real Provence in good company ...

someone to look up to

jean gill

If you are a dog-lover, try *Someone to Look Up To*. Based on true stories. It's a dog's life in the south of France. From puppyhood, Sirius the Pyrenean Mountain Dog has been trying to understand his humans and train them with kindness...

How this led to divorce he has no idea. More misunderstandings take Sirius to Death Row in an animal shelter, as a so-called dangerous dog learning survival tricks from the other inmates. During the twilight barking, he is shocked to hear his brother's voice but the bitter-sweet reunion is short-lived. Doggedly, Sirius keeps the faith.

One day, his human will come.

If you like historical novels, try the winner of the Global Ebooks Award for Best Historical Fiction, *Song at Dawn*.

1150 in Provence, where love and marriage are as divided as Christian and Muslim.

A historical thriller set in Narbonne just after the Second Crusade. On the run from abuse, Estela wakes in a ditch with only her lute, her amazing voice, and a dagger hidden in her petticoats. Her talent finds a patron in Alienor of Aquitaine and more than a music tutor in the Queen's finest troubadour and Commander of the Guard, Dragonetz los Pros.

Weary of war, Dragonetz uses Jewish money and Moorish expertise to build that most modern of inventions, a papermill, arousing the wrath of the Church. Their enemies gather, ready to light the political and religious powder-keg of medieval Narbonne.

SNAKE
ON SATURDAYS
A romance for our times

JEAN GILL

One of the best books I've read
this year - Nicolle, goodreads

If you like romance, try *Snake on Saturdays.*
'One of the best books I've read this year.' Nicolle, goodreads

Helen Tanner lives alone and likes it that way. She runs her own business, spends her evenings out with friends, and tries to think as little as possible about the tragedy she has left behind. Until, that is, a dark-haired vet walks into her shop and into her life.

Her first unpromising encounter with Llanelli vet Dai Evans turns into a tumultuous affair which brings about irrevocable changes for both of them. Dai becomes closer to his farming family, and helps them through the BSE crisis, while Helen is forced not only to consider a new future, but to face up to a troubled past.

If you like biographies and true war stories, try *Faithful through Hard Times.*

'A most unusual military history book. There are few military non-combatant accounts of life in the Second World War, fewer still from an Other Rank. Based on words and feelings recorded at the time it is probably unique.' - Don Marshall, Military History Enthusiast

This is not a WW2 memoir. It is a riveting reconstruction from an eye-witness account written at the time in a secret diary, a diary too dangerous to show anyone and too precious to destroy.

The true story of four years, 3 million bombs, one small island out-facing the might of the German and Italian airforces - and one young Scotsman who didn't want to be there.

If you like Young Adult that works for adults too; if you're left-handed or know a leftie, try *On the Other Hand*

A mix of gripping story with fascinating facts on left-handedness. Everyone should think left-handed - or so 14 year old Jamie thought when she tied her hand behind her back for a day-long protest in school, against persecution of left-handers over the centuries. Her best friend Ryan publicised their cause with a new series of articles in the school magazine but just when their campaign is going well, Ryan's Mum drags him off from Wales to live in America. There he faces bullying at its most deadly and Jamie has to live from one email to the next to know whether her friend is coping. Teachers' Resource materials available free from www.jeangill.com

A small cheese in Provence

cooking with goat cheese

Jean Gill

If you like food and France, try *A Small Cheese in Provence*

Provençal food for the brain as well as the table. Cheese information, recipes, stories and quotations in French, Occitan and English, with beautiful full colour photographs throughout. A must for cheese-loving Francophiles, who will discover the Picodon 'a small cheese in Provence' that even travelled into space on an Apollo mission.

*Cross Words Answer – **SORRY**

www.ingramcontent.com/pod-product-compliance
Lightning Source LLC
Chambersburg PA
CBHW052003220626
47052CB00004B/1071